1. Eugène Atget; *Rue Pigalle, à 6 h. du matin en avril 1925*, 1925; albumen-silver print; 7⅛ x 9⅜ in. (18 x 24 cm); The Museum of Modern Art, New York, Abbott-Levy Collection, partial gift of Shirley C. Burden. Copy print ©1997 The Museum of Modern Art, New York.

The images appearing in the ocher band
are not intended to illustrate the text,
but are designed to serve as an independent
photographic essay, surveying a broader
history of the crime scene aesthetic.

Scene *of the* Crime

Scene _of_ the Crime

Ralph Rugoff

With contributions by Anthony Vidler and Peter Wollen

Initiated and sponsored by the Fellows of Contemporary Art and
organized by UCLA at the Armand Hammer Museum of Art and Cultural Center

Published in association with The MIT Press
Cambridge, Massachussetts   London, England

Scene of the Crime is published in association with the MIT Press, Cambridge, Massachusetts, and London, England, on the occasion of an exhibition of the same title initiated and sponsored by the Fellows of Contemporary Art, Los Angeles, and organized by UCLA at the Armand Hammer Museum of Art and Cultural Center, Los Angeles, July 23–October 5, 1997.

Additional support for the exhibition has been provided by the National Endowment for the Arts, a federal agency.

Occidental Petroleum Corporation has partially endowed the Museum and constructed the Occidental Petroleum Cultural Center Building, which houses the Museum.

Editor: Karen Jacobson
Design: ReVerb (Somi Kim, Beth Elliott, & Jérôme Saint-Loubert Bié)
Indexer: Kathleen Preciado

Printed in Hong Kong by Oceanic Graphic Printing Inc.

Library of Congress Cataloging-in-Publication Data

Rugoff, Ralph, 1957–

   Scene of the crime / curated by Ralph Rugoff; essays by Ralph Rugoff, Anthony Vidler, Peter Wollen; initiated and sponsored by Fellows of Contemporary Art, Los Angeles, California.

      p. cm.

Catalog of an exhibition organized by UCLA at the Armand Hammer Museum of Art and Cultural Center.

Includes bibliographical references and index.

   ISBN 0-262-68099-8

1. Conceptual art—California—Exhibitions. 2. Visual communication—California—Exhibitions. 3. Crime scene searches in art—Exhibitions. I. Vidler, Anthony. II. Wollen, Peter. III. Fellows of Contemporary Art (Los Angeles, Calif.). IV. UCLA at the Armand Hammer Museum of Art and Cultural Center. V. Title.

N6530.C2R84 1997
709′.794′07479494—DC21   97-8079
                                                    CIP

Front cover: Edward Ruscha, *Los Angeles County Museum on Fire* (detail), 1965–68 (cat. no. 64).

Back cover & inside cover: Lewis Baltz, *11777 Foothill Boulevard, Los Angeles, CA* (detail), 1991 (cat. no. 7).

Page 1: Paul McCarthy; *Bossy Burger* (detail), 1993; mixed-media installation and video; collection of Hauser & Wirth, Zurich, Switzerland; courtesy Rosamund Felsen Gallery.

Pages 2–3: Anthony Hernandez, *Untitled (Landscapes for the Homeless #62)* (detail), 1990 (cat. no. 40).

Page 17: Paul McCarthy; *Painting a White Line on the Floor with My Face* (detail), 1973; photograph of a performance; courtesy Rosamund Felsen Gallery.

Page 23: Sylvie Fleury; *Sublimes (Chanel Eyeshadow)* (detail), 1992; mixed media; dimensions variable; courtesy Postmasters Gallery.

Page 59: Nam June Paik performing La Monte Young's *Composition 1960 #10* for Robert Morris at Fluxus International Festpiel neuester Musik, Wiesbaden, 1962; photograph of performance (detail); courtesy Holly Solomon Gallery.

Page 131: US Air flight 427 wreckage at airport hangar in Pittsburgh (detail).

2. Roger Parry; Untitled (view from room with open door and inverted portrait), c. 1930; gelatin-silver print; 9 x 6½ in. (22.9 x 16.7 cm); The Art Institute of Chicago, Julien Levy Collection, gift of Jean Levy and the estate of Julien Levy, 1988.157.67. Photograph ©1997, The Art Institute of Chicago. All Rights Reserved.

Contents

Director's Foreword

The Board of Trustees and staff of UCLA at the Armand Hammer Museum of Art and Cultural Center are pleased to be able to present Scene of the Crime, an exhibition conceived and guest-curated by art writer and critic Ralph Rugoff and sponsored by the Fellows of Contemporary Art.

Scene of the Crime looks at the work of thirty-nine California artists, covering the period from the mid-1960s to the present, which examines the world we live in through a deadpan or "forensic" aesthetic. Works such as Vija Celmins's Time Magazine Cover (Watts Riots) (1965), John Divola's Forced Entry series (1976), Jeffrey Vallance's Run Over Art Shipment (1990), and Anthony Hernandez's Landscapes for the Homeless series (1989–90) serve as a means of reassessing the ways in which we interpret the residue of events. In his extensive essay for this catalogue, Rugoff offers a unique perspective on how the development of this aesthetic parallels and reflects our cultural fascination with crime scenes and investigations, ultimately suggesting a pervasive skepticism toward "official" realities of any kind. In his lively essay Peter Wollen distinguishes Scene of the Crime from Paul Schimmel's ground-breaking exhibition Helter Skelter, presented at the Museum of Contemporary Art in Los Angeles in 1992, which included works by some of the same artists. Wollen states that, in contrast to the earlier exhibition, "Scene of the Crime is cold rather than hot, depressive rather than manic." One sees in these essays the seeds of a new approach to art criticism and appreciation.

Scene of the Crime could not have been realized without the strong support of the Fellows of Contemporary Art, who, as individuals and as a group, have proven to be the most reliable sponsors of exhibitions that feature the internationally prominent art

3. John Divola; Untitled (broken furniture), from *Broken Furniture and Evidence of Aggression*, 1995 (cat. no. 27).

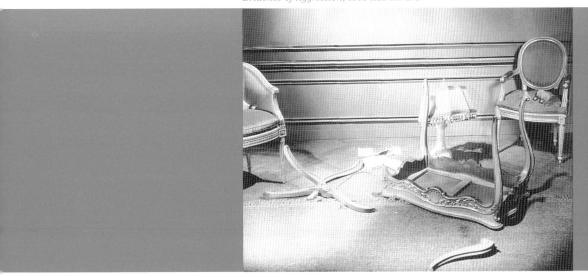

produced in California. The group's support is extended not only to exhibitions but also to the catalogues that accompany them, thus ensuring a lasting record of artistic accomplishment.

My special thanks also go to Elizabeth Shepherd, curator of the UCLA/Hammer Museum, and the curatorial staff for working with Mr. Rugoff and the Fellows through every step of the planning and presentation of this thought-provoking exhibition.

Henry T. Hopkins

Director, UCLA at the Armand Hammer Museum

Sponsor's Foreword

Humankind seems to be perversely fascinated with the scene of the crime and all that it suggests. From detective novels to film noir to TV news coverage of crime-in-progress, we get hooked. Is this magnetic attraction to nefarious activity the by-product of late twentieth-century, media-saturated urban (and suburban) life? Or end-of-the-century angst? Or just human nature, piqued?

The Fellows of Contemporary Art invites you to investigate a different kind of Scene of the Crime, an exhibition presented in cooperation with UCLA at the Armand Hammer Museum of Art and Cultural Center. This exhibition is the twenty-fifth sponsored by the Fellows since its inception in 1975. The mission of the Fellows is to nurture and present contemporary art of California by underwriting exhibitions featuring mid-career and emerging artists. Each exhibition is accompanied by a catalogue that provides scholarly documentation of the occasion and the work.

Although Scene of the Crime represents the first collaboration between the Fellows and the UCLA/Hammer Museum, our group has had a long-standing and fond association with Director Henry T. Hopkins, who has curated for the Fellows in the past. Mr. Hopkins's always gracious and astute guidance during this project has been much appreciated.

We give generous thanks to guest curator Ralph Rugoff, whose original premise has blossomed into a brilliant thesis and exhibition. His "forensic" eye has created a context that casts an interpretive light all its own, bringing to the surface interesting connections, ranging from the curiously peculiar to the sublime. Working with the Hammer Museum's curator, Elizabeth Shepherd, has been a pleasure. Her efficiency, resolve, flexibility, and good humor represent the evidence that has enabled this exhibition to be stamped "solved."

4. Claes Oldenburg; *Bedroom Ensemble*, 1963; wood, vinyl, metal, artificial fur, cloth, and paper; 118⅛ x 255⅞ x 206⅜ in. (300 x 650 x 525 cm); National Gallery of Canada, Ottawa.

Several among the Fellows who were instrumental in the planning and execution of Scene of the Crime deserve recognition. Thanks go to the immediate past chair, Diane Cornwell; to 1995's long-range exhibition planning chair, Kathy Reges, whose committee first selected Scene of the Crime; and to present chair Tina Petra, for helping to see the exhibition through to completion. Special thanks go to Linda Polesky, Fellows liaison to the exhibition, who relayed communication among all parties on the scene and provided enthusiastic and insightful reports. Finally, we gratefully acknowledge Administrative Director Carole Kim, who has gracefully orchestrated the multitude of details that such an exhibition entails.

Joan B. Rehnborg
Chair, Fellows of Contemporary Art

5. Frances Glessner Lee; *Dark Bathroom*, c. 1940s, from Nutshell Studies of Unexplained Death; mixed-media miniature diorama; collection of the Office of the Chief Medical Examiner, Baltimore.

Acknowledgments

My first thanks must go to the Fellows of Contemporary Art, without whose support this exhibition would not have been possible. Linda Polesky, who served as liaison, offered unqualified enthusiasm and reassurance, and the Fellows' two wonderfully able and unfailingly helpful coordinators, Alice Momm and Carole Kim, helped steer the project along from its earliest stages.

If debtors' prison still existed, my debt to the staff of the UCLA/Hammer Museum would no doubt result in a life sentence. Curator Elizabeth Shepherd's leadership, her unflagging optimism in the face of difficulties of all kinds, and her imaginative responses to them have set an example I will never forget. Assistant Curator Mary-Kay Lombino ingeniously solved every mystery regarding the whereabouts of the artworks in the exhibition; dealt with last-minute changes with equanimity, grace, and good humor; and provided invaluable feedback. In putting together the catalogue's photographic essay, Curatorial Assistant Claudine Isé tracked down hard-to-find images with the tenacity and resourcefulness of a brilliant investigator, pursuing the most obscure leads and inevitably, just when I had given up hope, finding what we were looking for. No challenge proved beyond her formidable skills.

For the catalogue, thanks go to Karen Jacobson, whose astute editing and ability to weather uncertain deadlines were much appreciated. The designer Somi Kim was, as always, both a pleasure to work with and a model of professional excellence.

Thanks also go to my fellow catalogue essayists: Peter Wollen, who has long provided an inspired example in detecting overlooked art-historical clues, and Anthony Vidler. Finally, I owe my unending gratitude to the usual suspects: the artists in the exhibition, so

6. Frances Glessner Lee; *Three-Room Dwelling*, c. 1940s, from Nutshell Studies of Unexplained Death; mixed-media miniature diorama; collection of the Office of the Chief Medical Examiner, Baltimore.

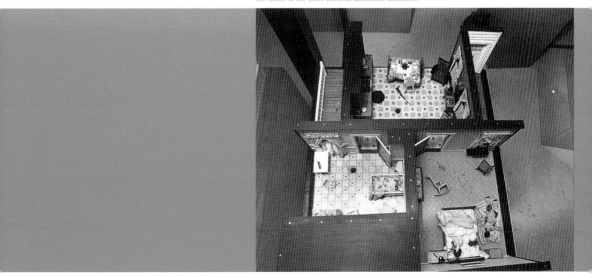

many of whom were generous with their time, both in showing me work that I was unfamiliar with and in discussing other artists whose work seemed relevant. I would also like to thank the many artists with whom I met who were not included in the exhibition (almost always for thematic reasons), as these meetings, an invisible part of the curatorial process, were also invaluable.

Ralph Rugoff

Guest curator

On behalf of the museum and its staff I would like to extend special thanks to the many contributors to this project whose enthusiasm and support have been critical to its successful completion. The lenders to the exhibition, whose names appear on page 154, have been particularly generous in responding to our requests for works of art. The artists and their gallery representatives have been equally cooperative, patiently answering our numerous queries. Authors Peter Wollen and Anthony Vidler have enriched this volume with their insightful essays. Roger Conover and Jane Brown at the MIT Press have been delightful colleagues and have provided us with an exemplary experience of catalogue copublication.

Our cosponsor in this venture, the Fellows of Contemporary Art, deserves our deepest thanks for bringing this exhibition to our attention and providing critical financial support for it. Past and current chairs Diane Cornwell and Joan B. Rehnborg, exhibition liaison Linda Polesky, and treasurer David Partridge—along with Linda Brownridge,

Maureen Carlson, and Stephen Kanter—offered their unstinting assistance throughout the planning and implementation of the exhibition. Carole Kim, the Fellows' administrative director, has been a joy to work with and has continually and calmly demonstrated her talents for meeting the unique demands of the collaborative process.

Scene of the Crime has enjoyed the support of the entire staff at the UCLA/Hammer Museum, including Associate Director Paula Berry, Chief Preparator Mitch Browning, Controller Patty Capps, Director of Education Cindi Dale, Development Associate Marpessa Dawn Outlaw, Publicist Stephanie Rieke, Bookstore Manager Maggie Sarkissian, and Development Director Amy Weinstein. Registrar Susan Lockhart has managed the complex job of coordinating loans and arranging shipping with her customary expertise and efficiency. Two colleagues have provided consistent inspiration and support from the outset of this project. Curatorial Assistant Claudine Isé's resourcefulness in obtaining the photographs for this publication has been truly remarkable, as has been her gracious assistance in all aspects of its production. Assistant Curator Mary-Kay Lombino has masterfully provided research support and cheerfully maintained the checklist under challenging conditions.

Outside the museum, Karen Jacobson is to be thanked for the superb editing of this catalogue, and Somi Kim, Beth Elliott, and Jérôme Saint-Loubert Bié, for its outstanding design. Finally, guest curator Ralph Rugoff's persistent interrogation of his subject matter and his engagingly deadpan humor have made this project a gratifying and enjoyable experience. We are deeply in his debt.

Elizabeth Shepherd

Curator, UCLA at the Armand Hammer Museum

7. Gordon Matta-Clark; *Bronx Floors: Threshole*, 1973; four black-and-white photographs; each 10¼ x 13¼ in. (26 x 33.7 cm); courtesy Holly Solomon Gallery, New York.

Introduction

Ralph Rugoff

Criminalistics is defined as the analysis of traces. Thanks in part to such highly publicized disasters as the bombing of the Oklahoma City Federal Building and the crash of TWA Flight 800, this once-arcane field has become a familiar one in the popular imagination. Most of us now have some notion of the forensic investigator who, working with the leftover rubble of an explosion or a few drops of dried blood on a car seat, attempts to answer the seven classic questions of any investigation: who, what, where, with what, why, how, and when?

In a not dissimilar manner *Scene of the Crime* aims to engage the viewer in a process of mental reconstruction. In surveying thirty-five years of West Coast art, this exhibition highlights artistic practices that suggest links to a forensic approach or address the art object as if it were a kind of evidence. These works emphasize the viewer's role as investigator while underscoring the cluelike and contingent status of the art object. Often they trace or reflect a history of prior actions and motivations.

In contrast to the real-life criminalist, we are not asked as viewers to reach a definitive finding or conclusion; instead, our search for meaning engages us in a goalless activity of speculation and interpretation, of tracing the links between our emotional responses and the ideas that arise alongside them or that may in fact be triggered by them. The study of these relationships, not the solution of a puzzle, is the pleasure we may pursue as viewers.

This exhibition is not designed for the dispassionate investigator. In the course of examining the art in *Scene of the Crime*, one may experience curiosity and horror as well as an appreciation of beauty or even sublimity. But whereas modern art's notion of sublime transcendence linked art to an eternal present, this strain of art inevitably invokes specific histories. And like an actual crime scene, it provokes a complex array of emotions, suggesting that our aesthetic and moral responses cannot always be neatly aligned. Neither absolutely joined nor irreconcilably separate, they may comprise semi-autonomous realms of experience, interlocking and overlapping at certain points, diverging at others.

Before pulling back the forensic tape, as it were, and moving on to our larger inquiry, there are two potential misunderstandings I hope to clear up. First, although much of the work in this exhibition alludes to misdeeds of one kind or another while invoking issues related to our cultural fascination with criminal investigations, it does not merely document or editorialize. The artists represented here do not pose as officers of morality who call attention to, and rhetorically police, various social misdeeds and injustices. Nor do they have much use for the well-worn (and surprisingly persistent) notion of the artist as cultural outlaw. Instead, their work involves us in an

8. Daniel Faust; *LINCOLN Theatre Chair*, 1987; Cibachrome print; dimensions variable; courtesy the artist.

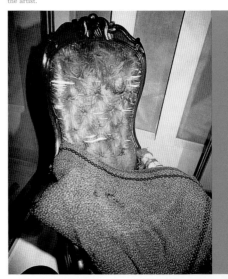

investigative process and evokes the crime scene primarily through its aesthetic of aftermath, as a place where the action has already occurred.

Second, although *Scene of the Crime* focuses on thirty-five years of West Coast art, the aesthetic it traces is limited neither to this time period nor to this place. Exploring a conceptual shift that began with action painting and the notion of the artwork as the aftermath of an event, this exhibition owes a debt to artworks made in Europe, Japan, and the United States, from the late 1940s through the present. It is in relation to this larger context that *Scene of the Crime* proposes to examine a significant development in the way we view contemporary art.

Limiting this show to work made in California was a technical requirement imposed by the initial funding group, the Fellows of Contemporary Art, but I never felt that this stipulation constituted a serious obstacle, as California-based artists have a long-standing and multifarious interest in what I have called a forensic aesthetic. There may be a couple of salient reasons for this. Hollywood, of course, has long enjoyed its status as the world capital of media violence, churning out countless scenes of criminal investigations for

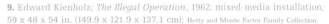

9. Edward Kienholz; *The Illegal Operation*, 1962; mixed-media installation; 59 x 48 x 54 in. (149.9 x 121.9 x 137.1 cm); Betty and Monte Factor Family Collection.

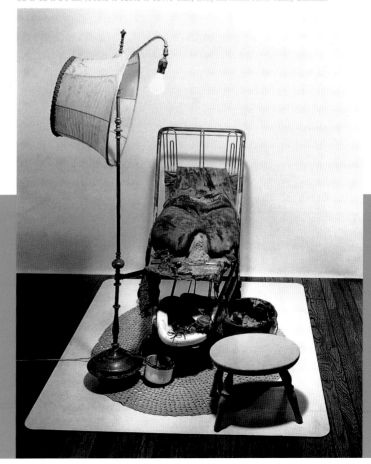

film and television. And in recent years Los Angeles County in particular has come to seem like our national crime and trauma center, thanks to a succession of sensational court trials, an urban uprising, and the much-publicized practices of drive-by shootings, car-jackings, and freeway slayings.

The art in *Scene of the Crime* engages us not only in reconstructing prior actions but also in tracing the play of promiscuously intermingled cultural codes that make reality itself seem suspect—a tradition with a significant history in our state.[1] Since the rise of Hollywood, Los Angeles itself has become suspiciously familiar; its streets and vistas seem to be composed of complex archaeological layers assembled from a farrago of TV episodes and films. In this richly sedimented environment—a kaleidoscope of hybrid fictions and competing modes of perception—"reality" evinces a patchwork quality that seems well suited to the criminalist's approach, with its allowance for contradictory fragments and missing details and its emphasis on traces.

In outlining the emergence of this aesthetic vein, which claims no movements or acknowledged champions, it has not been possible to construct a strict genealogy. I hope, however, that the evidence gathered in this exhibition and catalogue will raise a reasonable doubt about whether the usual versions of postwar art history tell the entire story, or whether any single narrative can. Part of the intent here is to shed light on a type of looking that seems characteristic of the present moment and to reexamine the idea, put forth by the French writer and artist Henri Michaux, that the artist is "the one who, with all his might, resists the fundamental drive not to leave traces."[2]

10. Bruce Conner; *COUCH*, 1963; mixed-media assemblage; 32 x 70¾ x 27 in. (81.3 x 179.7 x 68.6 cm); Norton Simon Museum, Pasadena, California, Museum purchase with funds donated by Mr. David H. Steinmetz III and an anonymous foundation, 1969.

Notes

1. Even before the development of the film industry, an
aura of uncertainty seemed to
hover around life in Southern
California, as though appear-
ances here were not to
be trusted: "There seems to
exist in this country something which cheats the
senses . . . which throws an
unreality around life," noted
Emma H. Adams, an early
visitor from Cincinnati (in
Carey McWilliams, *Southern
California: An Island on the
Land* [Salt Lake City: Gibbs
M. Smith/Peregrine Smith,
1973], 105).

2. Cited in Jean Baudrillard,
The Perfect Crime, trans. Chris
Turner (London: Verso, 1996), 1.

11. Robert Rauschenberg; *Bed*, 1955; combine
painting: oil and pencil on pillow, quilt, and sheet
on wood supports; 75¼ x 31½ x 8 in. (191.1 x 80 x
20.3 cm); The Museum of Modern Art, New York, gift of Leo Castelli
in honor of Alfred H. Barr, Jr. ©1997 Robert Rauschenberg / Licensed
by VAGA, New York, NY. Photograph ©1997 The Museum of Modern
Art, New York.

Vectors of Melancholy

Peter Wollen

Some years ago I acquired a much-used copy of a strange book called *Who Killed Robert Prentice?*, written by Dennis Wheatley, planned by J. G. Links, and published in London in the late 1930s for the Crime Book Society.[1] The unusual credit given for the planning of this book is explained as soon as you open it. Rather than a conventional narrative, it presents a carefully contrived dossier of evidence: personal letters (both typed and handwritten), press clippings, witness depositions, photographs, and so on. Central to the dossier is the documentation of the crime scene itself, the room in which Robert Prentice, a businessman with a harelip, was murdered (by his wife, it eventually turns out) and found sprawled on the floor next to the breakfast table, where he had just eaten a boiled egg. Among the documents collected in the dossier are a series of items

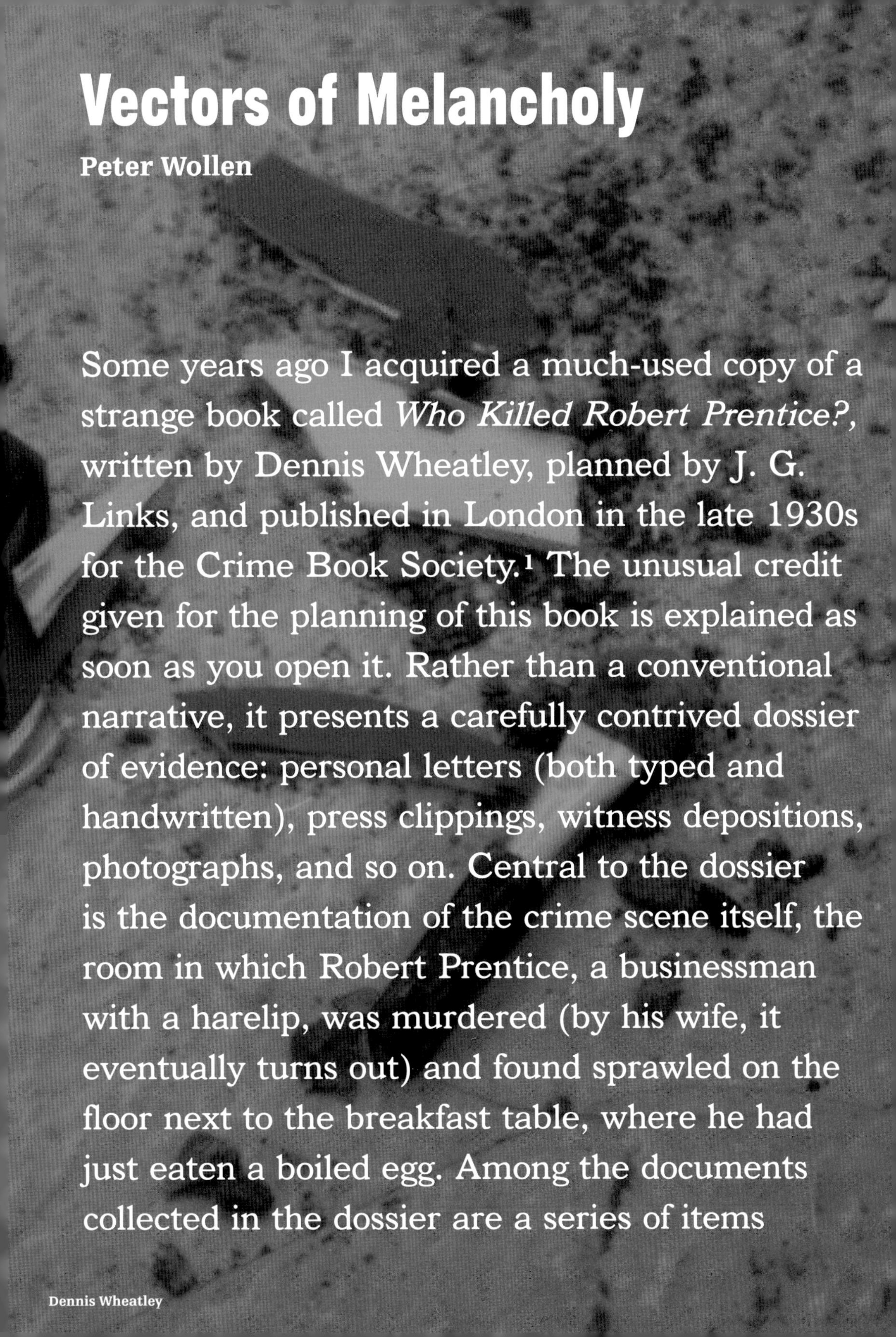

Dennis Wheatley

discovered at the scene of the crime, which took place in a weekend cottage belonging to the victim. The book contains, for instance, two police photographs (taken from different angles) of the kitchen of Whitedown Cottage, where the body was found, as well as a photograph of the adjoining bedroom and a number of other objects collected from the crime scene: a railway ticket in a cellophane envelope, a five-centime Belgian postage stamp, a photograph of the victim's mistress, a letter from the dead man to the mistress (still in its postmarked envelope), a photograph of the contents of the dead man's pockets (Sarnia matchbox, three used matches, fountain pen, calling card, bottle of bismuth dyspepsia tablets, three keys, some coins, a piece of paper with a license-plate number jotted down, and a long-term car-park ticket), as well as torn fragments of a photograph left in the garbage bin under the kitchen sink. The section of the book following page 100 is sealed with a gummed strip, and the reader is warned, "Do not break this strip until you have decided who you would arrest for the murder of Robert Prentice."

The scene of the crime is a fertile site for fantasy—morbid, fetishistic, and obsessive. The dominant paradigm for crime stories remains that of the obsessive investigator, seeking to restore meaning to a scene of traumatic chaos, thus warding off the underlying sense of panic brought about by violent and transgressive acts. Alongside this, however, we also encounter the fetishistic attraction of the crime scene exhibits themselves—matchboxes, bismuth tablets, eggcups—displaced signifiers of the crime. We share in the sadomasochistic enjoyment that the onlooker secretly imagines that both the perpetrator and the victim may have experienced, the site of guilty fantasy. Finally, there is the mesmerizing anxiety produced by contact with the abject and the uncanny,[2] the awareness of a scene, haunted by degradation and terror, which is insistently fascinating, which suspends time and freezes the spectator into immobility yet, in the final analysis, remains safely removed from reality.

Scene of the Crime is a show with three dimensions: forensic photography, deteriorated architecture, and the banalization of melodrama. Sometimes one or another of these dimensions comes to the fore—for instance, forensic photography in the real-life crime scene pictures shot by Janet Fries, deteriorated architecture in the models of abandoned and defaced Case Study homes presented by Sam Durant, banalization to an extreme degree in Uta Barth's *Blow-up*-like documentation of meaningless details. At other times all three elements are present in varying proportions, bringing an overall "look" or "feel" to the exhibition. Nevertheless, it directs us toward three very different ways of looking: those of the classical detective or investigator, the connoisseur of death and decay, and the automaton frozen outside historical time. While there are many plausible ways of linking or compositing these three looks, there are also persistent tensions between them.

In the essay "Forensic Photography," from his book *Circus Americanus,* Ralph Rugoff (the curator of the present exhibition) notes that, by striving to be impersonal, forensic photography takes on the quality of a ritual act.[3] At the same time it often has the uncanny effect of seeming to bring the dead back to life; because photography necessarily freezes time, it effaces the boundary

Fries figs. 20, 38; cat. nos. 31–32
Durant fig. 19, cat. no. 28
Barth fig. 21, cat. nos. 8–10

between life (activity) and death (stasis). The ritual quality of forensic photography is given an added power by the ritual characteristics of the crime scene
itself. Carefully delimited by police tape, the crime scene appears to us as
hallowed ground. Detectives and criminalists and photographers pad around it
like priests, carefully preserving the purity of the site as they execute their
grim liturgical duties, photographing, measuring, gathering. The forensic look
is a celebrant's look.

Anybody who watches Court TV knows that crime scenes should never
be disturbed. They should never be contaminated. They should never be
entered by unauthorized people. Nothing should ever be moved until it has
been photographed. Nothing should be touched except with gloves or other
protective materials. Nobody should tamper or interfere with anything in
any way. The crime scene should be controlled, guarded, and protected; it
should be preserved in its integrity, untainted. In fact, it should be treated
exactly as if it were sacred. In this context the photographer's camera is not
simply a recording device, but an officiant's ceremonial object, and the photograph itself can be regarded as a kind of icon or relic. Forensic photography,
by confronting us with death, takes us into a realm that is radically different
from the norms of everyday life, a realm that evokes a tangled web of associations—transgression, violation, defilement, fatality.

Crime scenes present us with both a surplus and a dearth of meaning. They
are full of the resonances of inexplicable dread and destruction. At the same
time they can appear stupidly banal and vacuous. As we enter the terrain
of the crime scene, we enter a world in which meaning seems overwhelming in
its presence yet strangely insubstantial. Something happened there that we
cannot quite grasp or understand. In our minds such a space seems a kind of
anti-space, a space of negativity which is extraneous to the ordered space
of everyday life. This anti-space is haunted. It is as if an alien had landed there

12. Daniel Spoerri; *The Pail Is Not Arman's! (La Poubelle n'est pas d'Arman!)*, 1961; mixed-
media installation; 17⅜ x 46⅞ in. (44 x 119 cm); courtesy the artist and Swiss National Library, Bern.

and left a weird message for us to decode, challenging us to make sense of things that seem odd and out of place, that usher us into a world in which evil has bubbled up to the surface and punishment has fallen inexplicably upon the innocent.

In this exhibition these crime scenes are located, for the most part, in desolate, abandoned, and deteriorated settings. Houses are falling to pieces. Walls are grim and blank or defaced and peeling. Spaces are empty or littered with debris or a scattering of cardboard boxes or what appear to be traps for vermin. Doors have been forced open. Glass is shattered. Rooms are depopulated. The architecture is ephemeral, like a film set, or dilapidated, like a ruin. It calls to mind crack houses and run-down public housing and derelict industrial estates. Such environments suggest a fundamentally entropic view of history, a world in which everything is grinding to a halt and beginning to fall apart. We are constantly reminded that human habitats are built upon the wilderness and that our occupation of them is still precarious.

It is immediately tempting to interpret this sense of entropy as yet another symptom of a typically fin de siècle dystopianism, a kind of negative millenarian attraction to the idea of "posthistoire," as it is called by contemporary theorists of the "end of history."[4] The rough beast is felt slouching toward us through the wreckage. It is as if the series of traces of catastrophe which make up this exhibition direct us toward some impending grand catastrophe that will afflict us on a mass scale. This sense of impending doom, however, is not narrativized. In fact, it is not really presented as meaningful, any more than the crime scenes themselves suggest any depth of meaning. The vision of these exhibits is emptied out, banalizing, attenuated. In comparison with an earlier Los Angeles exhibition, *Helter Skelter,*[5] which included work by some of the same artists, *Scene of the Crime* is cold rather than hot, depressive rather than manic. It depicts a world emptied of affect, a world whose meaning is irretrievable.

This effect is achieved not simply by adopting the neutral style of forensic photography but also by leaching away the significance of narrative point of view and subjectivity. There are four elementary subject positions that we can take up in relation to the scene of a crime: those of the detective, the criminal, the victim, and the onlooker. The detective sees the crime scene as a place of opportunity, the site of obsessive curiosity, observation, and interpretation. The criminal sees the crime scene as a place of ritual transgression, the site of manic enjoyment and accomplishment of evil. The victim, dead, sees nothing. The victim is blind. (Perhaps the victim is still there, inert, lifeless, hacked to pieces, stuffed in a trunk.) The onlooker sees the scene as a place of transient spectacle, the site of morbid fantasy and distracting shock. The exhibits in *Scene of the Crime,* however, are not coherently organized within this canonical structure of looks. They defy the conventional dramaturgy.

For the most part they reduce the melodrama of crime and violence to banality and futility. In this sense they are reminiscent of Alain Robbe-Grillet's project when he launched the French *nouveau roman* (new novel) in the 1950s. Robbe-Grillet's novels were marked by what is technically known as "internal focalization"—the story is told from within rather than from outside—but this focalization is impersonal, mechanical. As in this exhibition, it is as if the story were being told by a neutral observer, present within the scene of the narrative (often, in fact, a crime story), who functions there much like a camera or recording device, often dwelling obsessively on peripheral detail: "The heavy hand-rail of the balustrade has almost no paint left on the top. The grey of the wood shows through, streaked with tiny, longitudinal cracks. On the other side of this rail, a good six feet below the level of the veranda, the garden begins..." [6] Robbe-Grillet deliberately rejected "the archaic myth of depth" or any interest in motivation or psychology.

Alain Robbe-Grillet

Similarly, the artists in this show are mostly obsessed with surface description and a purely forensic delineation of the scene of action, rather than re-creation of the crime itself or its dramatic effects. The works refuse either paranoid interpretation (the detective's role) or narcissistic identification (the criminal's role) or even fetishistic enjoyment (the onlooker's role). Nor do they invite us to speculate much about the victim, who simply remains a blank. For the most part we are confronted with a depressive, even affectless view of the world. Occasionally, as in Paul McCarthy's work or that of Nayland Blake, there are traces of the manic glee that ran through *Helter Skelter*, but these works are in the minority. Crime scenes can be represented as grotesque, macabre, uncanny, even sublime. But in this show they are not even abject.

It is tempting to see this radical desemanticization as a symptom of urban (or perhaps suburban) culture in its postmodern manifestation—the collapse of the New Deal epoch, with its sense of a unified community and a welfare state, to be replaced, especially during the Reagan-Bush-Clinton years, by a deregulated market and a philosophy of competitive individualism, in which civil rights are reconceptualized as consumer options, in which winners win and losers lose. The culture accompanying this transition to our "Leaden

13. Fred Wilson; *Addiction Vitrine*, 1991 (detail); mixed-media installation; dimensions variable; courtesy the artist and Metro Pictures.

Age," as economic historians have called it, is one stripped both of depth and of any sense of meaningful narrative. Attempts to describe it have been reduced to discussing theme parks and desolate bunkers as the relevant points of reference. Put another way, we are offered a choice between two types of entropy and flight from history—the five-star hotel and the refugee camp. This show rejects the Hollywoodized culture of the tourist spectacle and prefers instead to dwell on the dismal landscape of the abandoned building and the makeshift shanty.

Walter Benjamin

Sixty years ago, in the mid-1930s, Walter Benjamin, writing about the work of Eugène Atget, argued that forensic photographs of crime scenes inherently produce a political response because they invite interpretation and analysis rather than aesthetic contemplation.[7] They are understood to be reliable sources of evidence of real historical events. Forensic photography, in this view, is intrinsically public. It runs counter to the kind of "aesthetic privatization" that Benjamin, much influenced at this point by Bertolt Brecht, was determined to demolish—the dramatic aesthetics of psychological identification and empathy. Benjamin called instead for an art stripped of any trace of Hollywood melodrama, and he chose Atget and the crime scene photograph as his counterexamples. The crime to which Benjamin referred, however, is undoubtedly a social crime, a political crime, rather than an individual incident or a human destiny. Atget's photographs have a "political significance" precisely because they provide evidence of public "historical occurrences."

In retrospect we can see the polarities that run through Benjamin's essay "The Work of Art in the Age of Mechanical Reproduction"—contemplation versus action, sight versus touch, aura versus use value, painting versus photography—as echoes of a distinction that he made earlier, in "One-Way Street" (1928), between the artwork and the document: "In the art-work subject matter is a ballast jettisoned during contemplation. The more one loses oneself in a document, the denser the subject matter grows. . . . The fertility of the document demands: analysis."[8] In this sense the document is the site of meaning and analysis. How, then, can it be stripped of significance and become blank, frozen outside history? In the first instance this is achieved by suppressing the image of actual human beings. Very few of the works in the present exhibition show the body of a victim. Otherwise, the closest we come to seeing or even imagining specific human beings is through relics of an artist's performances or through grotesque doll-like simulacra in the work of Blake and McCarthy.

In fact, the work in the show that brings us back directly to a sense of public history is Anthony Hernandez's series of photographs of the makeshift "homes" of Los Angeles's homeless. In the dialogue that prefaces his book *Landscapes for the Homeless* (published not in L.A. but in Hannover, Germany), Hernandez comments on the fact that most of his photographs were taken on the edges of the freeway, where overpasses or foliage give some kind of shelter. The freeways are the most privatized spaces in Los Angeles, full of individuals in cars, hurtling through a wasteland without any human contact, in a kind of parody of atomization and alienation. As Hernandez notes: "The photographs don't give you the sound of the freeway, the smell of rotten food and defecation.

Hernandez fig. 22, cat. nos. 38–40

Yeah, what is this place? The freeway system of L.A. A ribbon of life for the real city but a wasteland for the forgotten. And the idea that poverty is a private affair." And his interlocutor responds, "Privatization at degree zero."[9]

One of Hernandez's photographs shows simply a torn and battered cardboard box, flattened out, surrounded by crumpled bits of paper, lying on dry, matted grass. What is this evidence of? What are these scraps of garbage the traces of? The crime here is surely a crime with political significance. The perpetrator is the logic of untrammeled free-market capitalism, but, in a certain sense, it is also us, as citizens of a democratic society that has dismantled its safety nets and reduced its outcasts to a kind of human garbage. This is a different kind of crime scene from most of the others in the exhibition, a politicized crime scene. Hernandez's interlocutor reminds him at one point that "the received wisdom is that Atget photographed Paris as though it were a crime scene." Hernandez responds: "Could we say that about Atget's pictures? Was Paris worth photographing? Could I look at my own pictures and say 'was it worth photographing'? The answer is yes, because nobody else was looking."[10] Hernandez sees crime scene photography in terms not of the neutral forensic stare, but of being a moral witness, looking at things so that they can be reshown to those who would prefer not to look, who have habitually avoided looking.

It is the depopulation of Hernandez's sites, of course, that suggests the comparison with Atget. But perhaps Benjamin's reading of Atget was overly optimistic. Perhaps the removal of human beings from the landscape leads not toward analysis but toward a new mode of aesthetic contemplation precisely because there is no moral reason behind Atget's look but simply a documentary impulse to record. In fact, the surrealists themselves, whose own interest in Atget stimulated Benjamin's, described Atget as a producer of documents. "But what documents!" wrote poet Robert Desnos. "With the marvellous lens

14. Paul McCarthy; *Bossy Burger* (detail), 1993; mixed-media installation and video; collection of Hauser & Wirth, Zurich, Switzerland; courtesy Rosamund Felsen Gallery.

of dream and surprise, for thirty-odd years Atget photographed all of Paris. . . . Without ever conceding anything to the picturesque or the anecdotal, Eugène Atget fixed life itself."[11] Desnos and his cohorts detected in Atget's "documents" the traces of a strange, dreamlike city, a deserted city, frozen in time, eerily uninhabited.

Eugène Atget

The surrealists came across Atget's work by chance. He happened to live on the same street as Man Ray. In 1928 Albert Valentin wrote an article about Atget's photographs for *Variétés,* noting that "seen at closer range, these dead ends on the city outskirts registered by his lens constitute the natural theater of violent crime, of melodrama."[12] Valentin wrote this after seeing the collection of Atget photographs that Berenice Abbott, a friend of Man Ray's, had purchased after the photographer's death in 1927. Presumably this was the article that Benjamin had in mind when he first wrote that "not for nothing were pictures by Atget compared to those of the scene of a crime" in a review of Abbott's 1930 monograph on Atget.[13] What struck both Valentin and Benjamin was the sensation of the uncanny (Valentin's word) given by Atget's attachment to "extremely strange sites where seemingly nothing aroused any interest," which drew us nonetheless into a "beyond" that existed "in the margins, in the filigree, in the mind."[14] In other words, Atget's photographs provided a banal and uninteresting setting into which we could project our own images of violence and melodrama.

In this context we are reminded of the other great photographer associated with the crime scene, one who was the polar opposite of Atget: Weegee, whose relentlessly gripping Murder Victim series of 1940–43 remains the classic instance of what we might call "hot," as opposed to "cool," crime scene photography. Weegee arrived at the murder scene as rapidly as possible, with the police rather than the criminalist, before the tape went up, before the ground was declared sacred. These were a journalist's photographs, which, strangely like Atget's, have retrospectively been categorized as works of art. In fact, Weegee's New York played much the same role for artists of the succeeding generation that Atget's Paris did for the surrealists. Most people—certainly most people who frequent art museums—still see violence and disaster as abnormal, as disturbances and disruptions. Weegee, in contrast, observed: "Look what we endure. We're born, and right away we're headed for disaster."[15] His photographs reflect his conviction that violence and disaster are routine.

**Weegee
(Arthur Fellig)**

Weegee's images of the crime scene usually show not only a victim but also a crowd of curious onlookers. The onlookers represent, as Weegee would put it, those who have endured, who are both reminded of impending disaster by the body on the sidewalk and reassured that—so far, so good—they have themselves avoided or even overcome such suffering. They feel schadenfreude, pleasure in the sight of catastrophe, rather than guilt. Weegee's crime scenes naturally attract a crowd. The cardboard boxes that shelter the homeless, as Hernandez noted, do not. Murderers and robbers, by contrast, become celebrities. Television and newspapers are full of their exploits. Of course, it is not surprising that artists should be drawn to subject matter that is already in the

spotlight, to analyze it or refunction it. The works in this show, however, tend
to dehumanize crime; we rarely see the perpetrator or the victim, only the bare
scene, dismal and empty. The violence and melodrama, the human passions
that attracted Weegee, are gone.

Apart from Hernandez's photographs, Lewis Baltz's photograph of the site
of the Rodney King beating, and the pieces by David Hammons and Alexis
Smith, the bulk of the works in the exhibition are chary of suggesting that
they might bear some kind of social message. They follow Weegee in their
implication that, in his words, "I have no time for messages in my pictures.
That's for Western Union and the Salvation Army. I take a picture of a dozen
sleeping slum kids curled up on a fire-escape on a hot summer night. Maybe I
like the crazy situation, or the way they look like a litter of puppies crammed
together like that, or maybe it just fits with a series of sleeping people. But
twelve out of thirteen people looked at the picture and told me I'd really got a
message in that one, and that it had social overtones." Quick to disavow the
charge of political or social concern, he concluded, "I thought somebody was
kidding me at first."[16]

Weegee liked to present himself as just a hard-boiled reporter, but when it
came to the crunch, he fell back on aesthetic arguments—"the way they look"
and "fits with a series." The artists in *Scene of the Crime* come to the same
kind of position but from the opposite direction. They are trained, as artists, to
apply aesthetic standards—the way things look, the way things fit with a
series—but they also want to disavow the privileged status of art for their work
and claim instead something of the professionalism, cynicism, and opportunism,
even perhaps the negative aura, of the hard-boiled reporter unconcerned with
aesthetics. The result is a compromise: an aesthetics of blankness, an art of
vacancy. "X Marks the Spot" was the title Georges Bataille gave to an article
he wrote for *Documents* in 1930, a piece about a collection of forensic

Baltz fig. 23,
cat. no. 7
Hammons fig. 24,
cat. no. 33
Smith fig. 25,
cat. no. 67

15. Richard Serra; *Splash Piece: Casting (Gutter Cast—Night Shift),*
1969–70/1995; lead; 19 x 108 x 179 in. (48.3 x 274.3 x 454.7 cm); San Francisco
Museum of Modern Art, gift of Jasper Johns.

photographs of Chicago gangland murder victims.[17] For a later generation of artists the forensic gaze provides, at times, a kind of moral alibi, a displacement into the register of the connoisseur or the automaton, a fetishization of the spot rather than the act.

Once again we are reminded of Robbe-Grillet and the procedures of "writing degree zero" which Roland Barthes detected and praised in his work.[18] In an unexpected way what we find here is a new aesthetics of minimalism, applied not to abstract art, as in the past, but to a new genre of figurative art. It alludes to violence and melodrama while draining it of its significance, reducing its semantic charge to the bare minimum. This work is like an art-world shadow of the tabloid press or the Hollywood melodrama, sharing the same interest in violent crime but reducing it to a pretext for aesthetic asceticism and a paradoxical, perhaps ironic, postminimalism. It gives us the empty room, the broken pane of glass, the isolated object, the pile of debris. It eschews moralism and only hints at politics. It is an art of enigmatic traces, reduplicating the already enigmatic traces of the real-life crime scene.

This aestheticization of the neutral document has its roots in conceptual art, which itself developed out of minimalism. Conceptualism put the document at the center of contemporary art practice, ousting drawing and painting from their place of privilege. The conceptualist use of documentation itself derived from artists' historic move into performance, either private and procedural or public and theatrical. There is an ironic echo of this in John Baldessari's refashioning of the famous documentary photograph of Jackson Pollock performing as an action painter for the camera. Other artists represented in the show— Chris Burden, Barry Le Va, Ed Ruscha, Alexis Smith—have early associations with conceptual art. We begin to sense an eerie parallelism between conceptual art and forensic photography, in the way that each of them involves providing a neutral documentary record, and the performances neutrally documented in the work of Vito Acconci or Chris Burden could be as melodramatic and violent as almost any crime. By treating the performance as private and invisible to the public, by leaving as its trace only a series of neutral photographs, conceptual art seemed to push its refusal of aesthetics even further than minimalism.

Baldessari fig. 27, cat. no. 6

In this way the foundation was laid for a new kind of aestheticism, one that required a new kind of connoisseurship—an acute sensitivity to the trite, the futile, the banal, and the insignificant. This new aestheticism is one of atmosphere and of detail. By "atmosphere," I mean a sense of the uncanny or the abject as psychic spaces suggested by a work, by "detail," the need for fixation on a single item of interest. *Scene of the Crime,* for example, is full of tears, rents, holes, cracks, and gashes. This evidence of the puncturing of an envelope (carnal, architectural) is the signifier of a recurrent act of forcible entry. These rents and gashes and unravelings and crumblings are also signifiers of decay and collapse. What was once seen as hallowed ground, as a sacramental site, is no longer preserved intact and untainted, but deliberately polluted and violated.

Perhaps this parody of ritualization, this disenchanted reenactment, is itself an act of sacramental repetition, an attempt to overcome our crisis of under-

standing, to bring meaning back negatively. To repair a rip or gash in the fabric
of our assumptions about life, a moral unraveling and crumbling, we need
to reenact the rip and the unraveling in the guise of art. This approach carries
with it resonances of Nietzsche rather than Benjamin. It rejects both conventional morality and the idea of political and social change, preferring instead to
invoke the symbolic power of a primal defilement and violation. Looked at in
the context of the ideology of posthistory, the scene of the crime now takes on
a new resonance for us. The twentieth century is reconfigured as an epoch of
mass crime, traumatic violence, and ruthless exploitation. Seen from this
vantage point, we are leaving a century of war, crash, depression, segregation,
holocaust, nuclear annihilation, world domination, assassination, body bags,
junk bonds, underclass.

Ernst Bloch

As Ernst Bloch pointed out in his 1960 essay "A Philosophical View of the
Detective Novel," the peculiarity of the detective genre is that the crucial
dramatic action—the crime—always takes place before the story has begun.
It is narrated retrospectively, at the end, rather than presented directly, in the
beginning. Crime stories are always about memories and traces. They take
place in a world of recollection and ruin, a world whose dominant emotion is

16. Shozo Shimamoto; *Throwing Bottles of Paint*, 1956; performance at the second Gutai exhibition, Ohara-Kaikan, Tokyo, October 1956; courtesy Ashiya City Museum of Art and History, Japan.

always sliding toward melancholy. In the Christian view of the world history begins with a crime—Eve taking the apple from the tree—and every human event that follows takes place under the shadow of this original sin and the expulsion from Eden. In the Oedipus story the protagonist's parricide and incest take place before the action of the play begins. The whole concept of the scene of the crime implies a melancholy aftermath to follow. In an optimistic view of history, Bloch points out, this implies that "thus, the den of gangsters has erupted into the world of the righteous; it must be redressed and rendered harmless."[19]

But what if the crime cannot ever be redressed, what if the task of redemptive signification set for human history can never be completed? What if, as Bloch put it, "the world into which the reader has chanced" looks like "a cabinet of monstrosities, an inn of scoundrels, or an insane asylum"?[20] What if it looks like a detective story in which there is no resolution, no concluding scene in the drawing room when the detective assembles all the guests and solves the riddle, unmasks the murderer? What if crime simply generates chaos and senselessness? What if history has no redemptive task? What if it has no meaningful narrative? If the scene of the crime cannot be narrativized, if it can never be restored to the world of meaning and comprehension, then what else can it do but decay, crumble away, and become a ruin? And as we contemplate this ruin, with its eerie relics and its sinister holes and cracks, what else can we do except resort to melancholy? Traditionally artists have been forward-looking, in the vanguard, in search of solutions. They have helped us, in Jack Katz's phrase, "make socially constructive sense of suffering."[21] When this mission is exhausted, there is nothing left for artists to do except survey the scene of the crime with a sense of resigned melancholy. The classical investigator has become a connoisseur of decay and death, while the connoisseur, in turn, has become an automaton, frozen outside historical time. The vectors of melancholy are strangely reversed. We mourn for a meaningless future.

Notes

1. Dennis Wheatley, *Who Killed Robert Prentice?* (London: Hutchinson, n.d.). The last document in the book is dated May 31, 1937. This suggests that the book was published later in 1937, but no evidence has yet been found to confirm this hypothesis.

2. For the concept of "abjection," see Julia Kristeva, *Powers of Horror: An Essay in Abjection* (New York: Columbia University Press, 1982). For the concept of the "uncanny," see Sigmund Freud, "The Uncanny" (1919), in *The Standard Edition of the Complete Psychological Works of Sigmund Freud,* ed. James Strachey, vol. 17 (London: Hogarth Press, 1974), 217–52.

3. Ralph Rugoff, *Circus Americanus* (London: Verso, 1995), 183–86. Rugoff's essay stems from a visit to James Njavro, chief of forensic photography at the L.A. County coroner's office.

4. See Perry Anderson, "The Ends of History," in *A Zone of Engagement* (London: Verso, 1992).

5. Catherine Gudis, ed., *Helter Skelter: L.A. Art in the 1990s,* exh. cat. (Los Angeles: Museum of Contemporary Art, 1992). The exhibition was curated by Paul Schimmel and included work by Chris Burden, Mike Kelley, and Paul McCarthy.

6. Alain Robbe-Grillet, *Jealousy* (New York: Grove Press, 1965); originally published as *La Jalousie* (1957). See also idem, *Pour un nouveau roman* (Paris: Gallimard, 1963). For "internal focalization," see Gérard Genette, *Narrative Discourse* (Ithaca, N.Y.: Cornell University Press, 1980).

7. Walter Benjamin, "The Work of Art in the Age of Mechanical Reproduction," in *Illuminations* (New York: Schocken, 1969), 228.

8. Walter Benjamin, *One Way Street and Other Writings,* trans. Edmund Jephcott and Kingsley Shorter (London: Verso, 1979), 66.

9. Anthony Hernandez, *Landscapes for the Homeless,* exh. cat. (Hannover: DG BANK-Forderpreis Fotografie, for the Sprengel Museum, 1995), 13.

10. Ibid., 13.

11. Robert Desnos, "Eugène Atget," *Soir,* 11 September 1928, cited in Molly Nesbit, *Atget's Seven Albums* (New Haven: Yale University Press, 1992), 5.

12. Albert Valentin, "Eugène Atget (1856–1927)," cited in ibid., 196.

13. "Walter Benjamin's 'A Short History of Photography,'" trans. Phil Patton, *Artforum* 15 (February 1977): 46–51, discussed in ibid., 51. The monograph was organized by Abbott but is usually catalogued under Pierre Mac Orlan; see *Atget, photographe de Paris* (Paris: Jonquières; New York: Wehe, 1930). Mac Orlan wrote the introduction for both these editions.

14. Valentin, "Eugène Atget (1856–1927)," 196.

15. Cited in Peter Martin's introduction to the exhibition catalogue *Weegee* (San Francisco: San Francisco Museum of Modern Art, 1984), 11.

16. Ibid.

17. Georges Bataille, "X Marks the Spot," *Documents* 2, no. 7 (1930).

18. Roland Barthes, *Writing Degree Zero* (New York: Hill and Wang, 1968).

17. Eva Hesse; *Right After*, 1969; fiberglass; 60 x 216 x 48 in. (152.4 x 548.6 x 121.9 cm); Milwaukee Art Museum, gift of Friends of Art.

19. Ernst Bloch, "A Philosophical View of the Detective Novel," in *The Utopian Function of Art and Literature* (Cambridge: MIT Press, 1988), 260. Bloch wrote this essay in 1960, but it was not published until 1965 in his *Literarische Aufsätze* (Frankfurt am Main: Suhrkamp). At the time of writing, he was still living in East Germany, where he had been forced to retire and was banned from publishing or public speaking.
20. Ibid., 261.
21. Jack Katz, *Seductions of Crime: Moral and Sensual Attractions in Doing Evil* (New York: Basic Books, 1988). Katz argues not simply that the crime scene becomes a ritualized site, as Rugoff suggests, but that dread-inspiring crime itself is often a ritual act of defilement, whose site is chosen as such, "structured for cosmological transcendence."

18. Mike Kelley; *Untitled,* 1990; cotton blanket, yarn; 1¾ x 85¾ x 89¾ in. (4.4 x 217.8 x 228 cm); courtesy Rosamund Felsen Gallery.

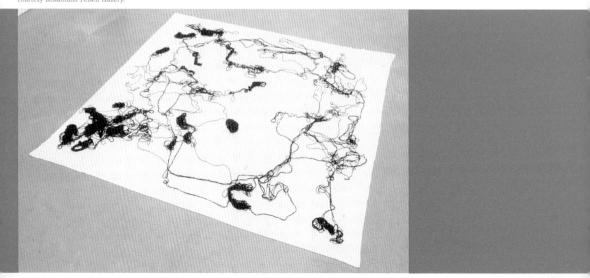

Plates

19. Sam Durant
Abandoned House #5, 1995
(cat. no. 28)

20. Janet Fries
Untitled (detail), 1975
(cat. no. 31)

21. Uta Barth
Ground #74, 1996
(cat. no. 10)

22. Anthony Hernandez
Untitled (Landscapes for the Homeless #62), 1990
(cat. no. 40)

23. Lewis Baltz
11777 Foothill Boulevard, Los Angeles, CA, 1991 (printed 1992)
(cat. no. 7)

24. David Hammons
Admissions Office, 1969
(cat. no. 33)

25. Alexis Smith
All the Simple Old Fashioned Charm, 1984
(cat. no. 67)

26. Edward Ruscha
Los Angeles County Museum on Fire, 1965–68
(cat. no. 64)

27. John Baldessari
White Shape, 1984
(cat. no. 6)

28. Bruce Nauman
Dead Center, 1969
(cat. no. 59)

29. John Divola
Los Angeles International Airport, Noise Abatement Zone,
Forced Entry (76FES29i), 1976
(cat. no. 23)

30. Robert Overby
Door with Hole, Second Floor, 4 August 1971, 1971
(cat. no. 60)

31. Barry Le Va
Shatterscatter (Within the Series of
Layered / Pattern Acts), 1968–71
(cat. no. 45)

32. Vija Celmins
Time Magazine Cover (Watts Riots), 1965
(cat. no. 19)

33. Bruce Conner
Prints, 1974
(cat. no. 21)

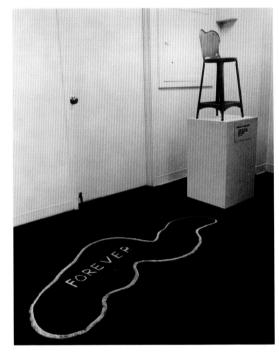

34. Chris Burden
Sculpture in Three Parts, 1974
(cat. no. 18)

35. Terry Allen
Memory House, 1973
(cat. no. 1)

36. Jeffrey Vallance
Cloth Penetrated by the Holy Lance, 1992
(cat. no. 71)

ROYAL

ROAD TEST

More than Meets the Eye

Ralph Rugoff

But is not every spot of our cities the scene of a crime?
—*Walter Benjamin* [1]

On August 21, 1966, a windless Sunday, under clear skies, Ed Ruscha drove two passengers down Route 66, cruising in a 1963 Buick Le Sabre at a speed of ninety miles per hour. At precisely 5:07 p.m. Mason Williams, the team's designated "thrower," tossed a Royal (Model "X") typewriter from the passenger window. After the car pulled off to the side of the road, photographer Patrick Blackwell documented the resulting wreckage.

Royal Road Test (1967), the sixty-two-page book Ruscha assembled from this "experiment" in destruction, has the look of a forensic manual. Deadpan black-and-white photos depict fragments of the shattered typewriter in situ, accompanied by laconically factual captions such as "Point of impact" or "Illustration showing distance wreckage traveled." Close-ups reveal a piece of the cylinder knob, a tab key ("photographed as found in a bush"), a section of the typewriter's back cover. Shown wearing white button-down shirts, Ruscha and Williams appear to be lab technicians in the field, examining the scene of an accident.

Ruscha fig. 47, cat. no. 65

In the same year Bruce Nauman began a series of works that recorded physical traces of absent structures or residues of prior activity. *Platform Made Up of the Space between Two Rectangular Boxes on the Floor* (1966) was the first of several sculptural works composed of casts of negative space. As if bluntly collecting raw data, Nauman also took impressions of various parts of his body as well as photos of his flesh pressed against a glass pane—a series of which culminated in images of oily impressions left on the glass like corporeal fingerprints. *Composite Photo of Two Messes on the Studio Floor* (1967), a black-and-white print of a sectional photo arrangement, shows the "non-art" debris left over from making sculpture. Evincing a criminalist's concern with traces, Nauman's image presents evidence of the artist's production process, reframed, however, as an artwork in itself.

Nauman fig. 49

At roughly the same time Barry Le Va, then a student at Otis Art Institute in Los Angeles, was already creating his Distributions, scattered works that betrayed the simple procedures by which they were created, such as cutting, folding, tearing, and throwing. Made initially from canvas, then from pieces of felt and ball bearings, these works consisted of vaguely interconnected components littered across an area of floor. By 1967 they had increased in dimension to room-size environments, so that the spectator viewed them by moving among the rubblelike fragments, attempting to reconstruct the overlapping decisions and concatenated actions that had produced this chaos.

Le Va fig. 37

Le Va's early work prods the viewer into an investigator's role and was often discussed in terms borrowed from mystery novels. *Shatterscatter (Within the Series of Layered/Pattern Acts)* (1968–71)—a stack of five glass sheets on the floor, each shattered by a hammer blow—echoes that genre's familiar structure: a past action (the serial fracturing of the glass) must be reconstituted through an investigation of its residue and speculation about its maker's motivations. The art object has become a set of clues.

Le Va fig. 31, cat. no. 45

All of the works that I have described confront us with the residue or record of an earlier event on which their meaning seems utterly contingent. Indeed, the art functions almost in a documentary fashion, conveying information about a set of prior actions or a missing body, so that the final work seems defined as much by an absence as by its own physicality.

This shared concern with documenting the aftermath of an activity, especially in the case of Ruscha, is often related by art historians to the evolution of conceptual art, yet this approach reached its early rhetorical climax in the late 1960s with the rise of the postminimalists, among whom Le Va and Nauman were initially grouped. Postminimalism—whose exponents included

Eva Hesse, Lynda Benglis, Robert Morris, and Richard Serra—was aptly described in a 1969 review by Max Kozloff as "sculpture which appears to be some kind of leaving . . . a symbol of an action process, about to be commenced, or already completed."[2] The work's production process was typically celebrated as its primary content, sometimes to the point where distinctions between sculpture and performance seemed to blur.[3]

With the reproduction of Le Va's work on the cover of *Artforum*'s November 1968 issue, these ideas quickly gained currency in the art world. But there was another, perhaps more significant aspect of this work which received less attention: in the words of critic Robert Pincus-Witten, "the virtual content of the art became that of the spectator's intellectual re-creation of the actions used by the artist to realize the work in the first place."[4] The audience, in other words, could no longer be mere viewers but had to function like detectives or forensic technicians, attempting to reconstruct the activities and ambiguous motivations congealed in physical artifacts. And, as at a crime scene, one encountered a diffuse field of clues rather than a coherently organized object.

Such work requires a different kind of scrutiny than that given to the conventional art object with a figure-ground orientation. It demands a scanning gaze able to sift through the details of a scene, to shuffle fragments of information that seem only haphazardly related. To some extent this new way of looking made up the content of Ruscha's *Royal Road Test*. That this "test" was performed on a typewriter, a machine that produces decipherable characters in the service of intelligible discourse, does not seem incidental, nor does the brand name Royal. In smashing this machine to meaningless rubble, Ruscha acted out the violent demise of several symbolic systems that comprised "royal" hierarchies of one kind or another—not least among them the supremacy of language as a medium of communication.

37. Barry Le Va; *Continuous and Related Activities; Discontinued by the Act of Dropping,* 1967; felt and glass; dimensions variable; Whitney Museum of American Art, New York, purchase with funds from the Painting and Sculpture Committee, 90.8a–b.

Appropriately, Ruscha's test report was presented in a high-speed, informa-
tion-heavy, picture-text format that reflected the rise of image-based media.
The black-and-white photos in *Royal Road Test* boast of an abundance of
detail, evidentiary values, and raw "factuality" that a simple written account
could never offer. Furthermore, Ruscha's work took the form of a mass-
produced book: no precious original, it was a common object circulating in the
world, a thing among things, stripped of the art object's aura of rarity.

By 1966, of course, painting itself had at times achieved similar status.
Once the presiding royalty of the arts, it had been subject over the preceding
two decades to a fate not unlike that of Ruscha's typewriter. No longer necessarily a window onto or model of the world (whether external or internal), it
had been reduced to a mere object that was slashed, shot at, placed facing the
wall, onto which paint was poured or objects and debris casually attached.
Having lost its transcendent position, painting had become an artifact in need
of a forensic reading.

The works by Ruscha, Nauman, and Le Va that I have mentioned are clearly
about more than meets the eye; in Le Va's words, such art insists that "content is something that can't be seen."[5] As already noted, it requires that the
viewer arrive at an interpretation by examining traces and marks and reading
them as clues. In addition, it is marked by a strong sense of aftermath: indeed,
much of Le Va's early work is known today only through photographs, and
like documents of a crime scene, these images present us not with a set of
objects so much as a place where *something happened*. Inextricably linked to
an unseen history, this type of art embodies a fractured relationship to time.
Like a piece of evidence, its present appearance is haunted by an indeter-
minate past, which we confront in the alienated form of fossilized and frag-
mented remnants.

This approach to art making embraces what I shall call a forensic aesthetic.
By "aesthetic," I do not mean a set of common formal concerns; like those
already discussed, the works in this exhibition do not share a definable visual
style. What links them is the type of approach they demand from their audience. Taken as a whole, this art puts us in a position akin to that of the forensic
anthropologist or scientist, forcing us to speculatively piece together histories
that remain largely invisible to the eye.

Since the early 1960s the influence of this aesthetic has been widespread,
manifesting itself in diverse types of work, from conceptual art to installation.
An inquiry into this peculiar "case," then, may not only shed light on a historical shift in the way we approach and interpret contemporary art but may also
tell us something about the emergence of a certain social gaze, a way of looking that is embodied in these works.

As with any investigation, one of the difficulties of this task is the tempta-
tion to make things fit, to squeeze clues into a coherent picture by highlighting
some facts and excluding others. Any competent detective must be suspicious
when evidence falls too neatly into a pattern. It will be necessary, therefore, to
look at different, often parallel threads of development and trajectories of

motive. There is every chance that at the conclusion of our search we may
be no more certain than we were at the outset regarding our object of inquiry.
The goal here, however, is not to uncover some absolute truth, but to pose
new questions about the history of postwar art and to tease from the familiar
ones a few intriguing and overlooked clues.

The Usual Suspects

"It looks like one of Bill's paintings."
—*Patricia (Sarah Miles) in Michelangelo Antonioni's* Blow-up *(1966), comparing a photo enlarge-
ment of a murder victim with her husband's abstractions.*

In reviewing early work by postminimalists who scattered their materials
around the exhibition space, both Kozloff and Morris cited the gestural,
"allover" idiom of abstract expressionism as a precedent.[6] Morris went on
to trace to the work of Jackson Pollock, and the later "stain" paintings of
Morris Louis, a concern with reincorporating process into the artwork itself.
"Their 'optical' forms resulted from dealing with properties of fluidity [of
paint] and the conditions of a more or less absorptive ground," he observed,
pointing out that the forms of their work "were not *a priori* to the means."[7]

This focus on process elides a more radical shift that had occurred with
Pollock's drip pictures, toward what the critic Harold Rosenberg famously
termed "Action Painting." "At a certain moment," Rosenberg wrote, "the canvas began to appear to one American painter after another as an arena in
which to act—rather than as a space in which to reproduce, re-design, analyze
or 'express' an object, actual or imagined. What was to go on the canvas was
not a picture but an event."[8]

38. Janet Fries, *Untitled* (detail), 1975 (cat. no. 32).

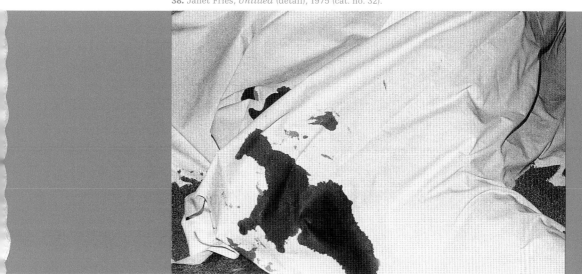

39. Carolee Schneemann; *Up to and Including Her Limits*, 1973–76; photograph of a performance; courtesy the artist.

While Rosenberg's claim has often been dismissed as a rhetorical flourish—
a work of art is not an action, ultimately, but an object—it needs only slight
modification to make perfect sense: what ended up on the canvas was not an
event, but its aftermath. Of course, one could argue that this is true of any
work of art, but the splatters, arcs, and loops of Pollock's drip paintings sug-
gestively recalled the dancelike movements with which they were made. And
because he worked on the floor, his canvases ended up collecting evidence of
everyday life: cigarette butts, small keys, bits of studio debris.

This notion of the picture plane as an arena of evidence marks a conceptual
shift in modernism, a movement away from consideration of an autonomous
art object to a growing focus on works or environments that bear the imprint
of prior activities—traces, as it were, of an unseen history. If the canvas could
not truly be considered "a moment" in the adulterated mixture of the artist's
life, as Rosenberg declared with his usual existential pitch, it did appear as a
kind of platform or stage on which a certain life had been lived.

Or spilled. Like blood splatters at a crime scene, "Jack the Dripper"'s
paintings recall a history of aggressive movements, and to see them as suggesting bodily spillage—as a number of critics have—does not seem unreasonable.
"Pollock treated his medium as analogically connected to his body and to the
unconscious as he understood it," David Humphrey has noted. "The loose
unstretched canvas that he worked on the floor became a stained sheet onto
which Pollock leaked himself."[9]

But of what punctured self, what riddled corpse, did the canvas offer evidence? Is it too much of a jump to recall that 1945 had unveiled the grimly
fascinating specter of atomic annihilation, and the possibility that bodies
could be transformed into convulsing skeins of matter by a blinding and all-
powerful energy? This was no doubt a crisis point in the history of modernism: indeed, the atom bomb had become an ultimate symbol of modernity,
alongside the Nazis' factory-style death camps. Under such extreme circumstances how could the body not appear as a potential forensic artifact? And
the art object itself, set adrift in an increasingly bureaucratized culture domi-
nated by mass-media circuses, seemed as deracinated and dislocated as any
article of evidence.

The influence of Pollock's approach, and its broader implications, spread
like a slow-moving stain across the fabric of postwar art. In Europe Lucio   Fontana fig. 63
Fontana's slit monochrome canvases, which he began producing in the early
1950s, seemed to further elaborate a forensic aesthetic, though under the
guise of late-modernist formalism. The skin of the canvas in these paintings is
slashed and violated, a classic avant-garde gesture aimed in part at the pictorial tradition of illusionism. With his piercing strokes, the artist heroically punctured the stale modalities of clichéd experience, exposing "reality"—the
gallery wall behind the canvas as well as the painting's own objecthood. At the
same time his action transformed the canvas into the relic of a knifing.

Pollock's legacy developed a more directly performative accent in the work
of artists associated with the Zero Society and Gutai movement in Japan during the early and mid-1950s. At roughly the same time that Fontana was pro-

ducing his slit monochromes, Shozo Shimamoto began his Hole Series (1950), cutting through the surface of paintings, which then functioned as a record of his physical interaction with his materials. In Shimamoto's later works made by throwing bottles of paint and in Saburo Murakami's *Work Painted by Throwing a Ball* (1954), Gutai-associated artists emphasized an aggressive process that produced not an abstract image per se, but traces that reflected specific material dynamics: angle and force of impact, viscosity of pigment, tension of surface area. "When the material remains intact and exposes its characteristics, it starts telling a story," stated Gutai founder Yoshihara Jiro.[10]

Shimamoto fig. 16

Murakami fig. 62

In the West a perfume of violence hovered over many works that incorporated signs of their production. Robert Rauschenberg's *Bed* (1955), a quilt and pillow splattered with paint, disturbingly extended the violent gestural strokes of abstract expressionism into a zone of domestic vulnerability. Savagely besmirched, the bed evoked an arena of prior turbulence, even terror. Because Rauschenberg's relationship with Jasper Johns dates from this period, *Bed* has been interpreted as an homage to their shared passion, yet it is one that calls to mind Georges Bataille's remark that copulation is a parody of crime. More than one viewer, as Leo Steinberg noted, said that it looked as if an axe murder had been committed in it.[11]

Rauschenberg fig. 11

Even Yves Klein's ironic *Anthropometries of the Blue Period* (1960), in which naked female models covered in blue pigment pressed themselves against prepared canvases, indirectly evoked the blood stains of murder victims. (As with paintings Klein made with a blow torch, the final canvas was mainly of interest as a forensic article, evidence of its own spectacular production.) Elsewhere the idea of art as a residue of violent activity took more literal forms: as if responding to Johns's target paintings, in 1961 Niki de Saint Phalle began a series of works made by shooting containers of paint, which bled onto her canvases and assemblages. Yoko Ono's performance script for

Klein fig. 61

Saint Phalle fig. 65

41. Police evidence photograph; courtesy City of New York, Department of Records and Information Services, Municipal Archives.

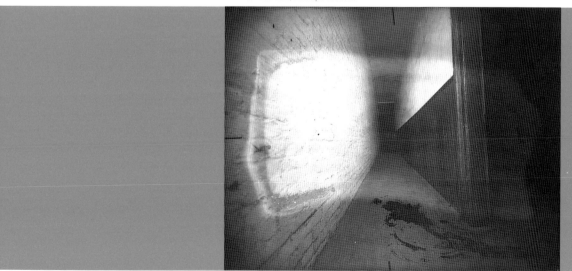

Painting to Be Stepped On (1960) featured instructions to "leave a piece of canvas or finished painting on the floor or in the street," suggesting the art-work as both the scene, and trace, of a future accident.[12]

By 1966, the same year that Ruscha carried out his experiment on a Royal typewriter, this line of inquiry reached a climax of sorts with the "Destruction in Art Symposium" in London, which brought together approximately eighty artists from twenty countries, including members of the Viennese Actionists, Ono, and Gustav Metzger. During the symposium Ralph Ortiz dismantled a piano with a sledgehammer; an artist named Pro-Diaz ignited pyrotechnic powders on three large painted surfaces; and Welsh artist and lecturer Ivor Davies produced an "explosion-happening" by blowing up movie posters and paper cutouts in a store window. One reviewer reported that "the explosions were almost strong enough to break windows and instilled fear."[13]

Whatever its overt object, the aggression in these works is clearly aimed at the idea of art. It reflects a convulsive cultural nihilism, somewhat gleefully predicated on the idea that, by destroying art, one could pass beyond its con-temporary spiritual bankruptcy to a more genuine experience. In a scheme where a work achieves authenticity only through its destruction, the "true" art object is necessarily forensic in character.

Hints of destructive or tumultuous activity also colored works by postmini-malists, such as Serra's splashed-lead pieces and some of Le Va's Distributions. Besides incorporating shattered glass, torn fabric, and even bullet shells, Le Va's works obliquely invited violence from the viewer, who had to pass directly through their scattered remains and so could easily, and inadvertently, disturb their placement. His chaotic installations conjured another order of violence as well. As Brian O'Doherty remarked in *Inside the White Cube*, "classical avant-garde hostility" expresses itself not merely by instilling physical discomfort but also by "removing perceptual constants": "In these arenas [the audience] assays what quotas of disorder it can stand." Or, as Jane Livingstone noted in an article on Le Va: "People are noticeably uncomfortable in the midst of these accumulations of debris. . . .What happens to the spectator's perceived relation-ship to his environment when it is made to appear chaotic in one degree or another is the essence of what Le Va's recent work is about."[14]

Serra fig. 15

What happens to the spectator, at least in part, seems to be an experience of fear, as if, surrounded by chaos, one's reassuring belief in a moral and ratio-nally ordered universe was rudely imperiled. This feeling is inextricably relat-ed to the sublime: as far back as the eighteenth century, aesthetic theorists such as Giambattista Vico and Edmund Burke argued that our experience of sublimity derived from primitive emotions such as terror. The threat of danger or pain was far more powerful than the promise of pleasure, and so the sub-lime had a more potent effect on the observer than the beautiful.

Yet evidence of disarray or violent aftermath may also elicit responses other than awe, such as curiosity or a melancholy wonder. Discussing the desired effect of his installations, Ilya Kabakov has said that he imagines "a viewer who is standing before a broken vase and thinking: 'This vase existed, and now it is no more. Why did it break? Was it a good vase?'"[15]

42. Judy Chicago; *Menstruation Bathroom*, 1972; mixed-media site installation at Womanhouse (1995 reconstruction); dimensions variable.

Evidence of prior turbulence may also provoke a sympathetic urge to reproduce it, as though violence were contagious. In 1969 British writer J. G. Ballard organized an exhibition of three crashed cars at London's New Arts Lab; over the course of a month visitors overturned one of the cars and broke every intact piece of glass in the others, while covering them with graffiti.[16] In that same year a Stanford University psychologist carried out a famous experiment involving vandalized cars, which suggested that "disorder invites even more disorder—that a small deviation from the norm can set into motion a cascade of vandalism and criminality." He called his theory, appropriately enough in regard to Le Va's work, the "broken window hypothesis."[17]

Perhaps, then, as cultural historian Joel Black has observed, it is no mere coincidence that the word *aesthetics* was introduced into English (from German philosophy) in Thomas De Quincey's 1827 essay "On Murder Considered as One of the Fine Arts." The aesthetic may be less a transcendent mode of every-day experience than a violent disruption of conventional "reality."[18]

It was this notion of conventional reality that Chris Burden aimed to disrupt in his November 19, 1971, performance *Shoot*, which brought at least one trajec-tory of the forensic aesthetic to its logical conclusion. At 7:45 p.m. he stood in an empty gallery in Santa Ana, California, and was shot in the left arm by a friend. The rifle was fired at a distance of approximately fifteen feet. The bullet is listed in Burden's spare text on the piece as "a copper jacket 22 long rifle."   **Burden** fig. 92

To O'Doherty there was something "infinitely pathetic about the single fig-ure in the gallery, testing limits, ritualizing its assaults on its body, gathering scanty information on the flesh it cannot shake off."[19] Violence in art—previ-ously directed against culturally loaded objects such as a typewriter, piano, or painting—was here coolly aimed at the artist himself, as if his ultimate fate lay in his transformation into a forensic artifact. Indeed, Burden's performance suggested a laboratory testing procedure, an inquiry into the reality of physical experience amid a media-saturated culture.

From another perspective Burden's act could be read as an intrusion of violence into the quasi-theological space of the gallery, the "white cube" that symbolized a manicured and hygienically manufactured reality. Given the general and then highly visible background of the Vietnam War, *Shoot* indi-rectly raised questions about who was considered suitable for shooting, that is, which segments of society could be routinely set up as cannon fodder by the U.S. military.

In addition, *Shoot* addressed the role of the audience, conspicuous here in its absence. Burden allowed no spectators in the gallery, insisting that his art be reconstructed only from the limited photographic evidence he presented afterward. Viewers were thus rendered voyeurs at one remove—a distanced relationship to violence that many Americans had already experienced thanks to the pervasive and graphic television coverage of atrocities in Vietnam. Should home viewers grow guilty about the vast gulf separating them from the spectacle of others' suffering, the avant-garde artist provided a means of atonement. As O'Doherty caustically noted, punishment of the spectator was a theme of advanced art; indeed, "perhaps a perfect avant-garde act would be to invite an audience and shoot it."

Burden had himself shot instead, substituting his own body for those of his absent audience. To O'Doherty this was a spectacular rhetorical twist: "Eliminating the spectator by identifying him with the artist's body and enacting on that body the vicissitudes of art and process is an extraordinary conceit. We perceive again that double movement. Experience is made possible, but only at the price of alienating it."[20] This "double movement" produces a type of art that seems to demand a forensic approach. Indeed, it may prove to define the very territory from which such an aesthetic emerges.

The Incident Room

The stuff lying around the object . . . grew more important than the object itself.
—*Barry Le Va*[21]

Le Va's remark sums up a perception that, in different ways, characterized a number of movements in the 1960s and informed the development of what eventually became known as installation art, arguably the preeminent format of the last decade. If we forget this legacy for the moment, however, we may better grasp the initial strangeness, the odd break, that this notion once represented. Why was it, after all, that the outlying "stuff" should somehow become more significant than the art object itself, that meaning came to reside less in a discrete entity than in a disordered and dispersed array?

At least one vector of investigation leads back to the development of an "aesthetics of objecthood" and its theatrical side effects. Fontana's slashed

43. Cady Noland; *Bloody Mess*, 1988; mixed-media installation; dimensions variable; collection of Andrew Ong; courtesy the artist and John Gibson Gallery, NY.

monochrome paintings of the early 1950s stand out as an early benchmark in this history: the slit in these canvases betrayed the work's status as an object and allied it with the architecture it revealed. Made a few years later, Johns's flag and target paintings, as Robert Morris observed, extended this principle: "[Johns's] works were not depictions according to past terms which had, without exception, operated within the figure-ground duality of representation. Johns took the background out of painting and isolated the thing. The background became the wall."[22]

In other words, by removing any kind of figure-ground relationship, Johns recast the gallery wall, the field of real space, as a pictorial element. The result was a theatrical doubling of identity—not only of the artwork, which appears as both image and object, but also of the gallery environment itself, which is no longer a mere container, but a key aesthetic ingredient. This aesthetic shift would later reach a rhetorical climax with minimalism, which presented the art object as a tool for structuring an aesthetic experience of space. Writing in 1966, Allan Kaprow also noted the gallery's altered role but linked it to the evolution of collage and assemblage. "Once foreign matter was introduced into the picture in the form of paper, it was only a matter of time before everything else... would be allowed to get into the creative act, *including real space*." By dissolving the boundaries of painting, he added, assemblage revealed that "the room has always been a frame or format too."[23]

That art's content now included the viewer's milieu meant that spectators no longer simply looked at, or into, a work so much as they were immersed and inscribed within it. Kaprow, who developed this principle in his Happenings, traced it back to Pollock: "Pollock spoke of being in his work while he painted.... With a little work a spectator before the finished painting could feel into the same state of immersion. But in the case of Environments, there is no question that one is inside and, for better or worse, a real part of the whole."[24]

44. Kazuo Shiraga; *Challenging Mud*, 1955; performance at the first Gutai exhibition, Ohara-Kaikan, Tokyo, October 1955; courtesy Tokyo Gallery, Japan.

The aesthetic of immersion, later elaborated by postminimalists such as Le Va and installation artists such as Edward Kienholz, drastically altered the conventional viewer-object romance. There was no longer an ideal viewing position, an objective perspective; instead, one's every glance was subjectivized. Rather than standing in frozen contemplation, the viewer embarked on an ambulatory investigation, wandering, occasionally pausing, gradually gathering data, and at the same time recollecting and comparing things seen a moment before.

This process clearly foregrounds the relativity of the viewing experience, but it is not only a question of physical perspective. "The context that has taken on so much importance is as much as anything the entire cultural predisposition of the viewer," O'Doherty observed, referring to our readiness to experience objects displayed in a gallery as "art."[25] Yet a crucial dimension of the forensic aesthetic is that it prompts us, as Kabakov noted, to ask how a given situation came about, to wonder what unseen circumstances produced the evidence before us. In arousing our curiosity, it may further lead us to examine the public aspects of our personal response, to consider the cultural biases that inflect and inform our interpretations; indeed, the word *forensic* derives from the Latin *forum*, with its attendant meaning of public discussion and debate.[26]

In many of Kienholz's tableaux and walk-in environments, including *Roxys* (1961–62) and *The Illegal Operation* (1962), which bluntly relate physical violence to specific social circumstances, the forensic aesthetic clearly opens onto public territory. These works do not document prior activities per se but conjure terminally played-out scenes, sites of postmortem investigations, and so reek of a forensic aura, inviting us to immerse ourselves in a theater of grisly clues, the aftermath of socially engineered horrors.

Kienholz fig. 9

Much cooler in attitude, Vija Celmins's drawings and paintings from the mid-1960s often focused as well on images of public violence. With the impersonal precision of a forensic sketch artist, Celmins depicted smoking revolvers, a

45. Cindy Sherman; *Untitled #167*, 1986; color photograph; 61⅛ x 91⅛ in. (155.3 x 231.5 cm); courtesy the artist and Metro Pictures.

car riddled with bullet holes, burning aircraft. Her subjects were often lifted from news photos; working in a serenely muted grisaille, she painted *Time* magazine's 1965 cover story on the Watts riots. In *Hiroshima* (1968), a graphite Celmins fig. 48 drawing of a shattered postatomic landscape, she portrayed each piece of rubble with relentless exactitude, and the hundreds of tiny marks on paper, made over long stretches of time, implicitly refer us back to the making of the image itself.

Like many of Celmins's pictures, *Hiroshima* evinces an almost evidentiary tone. It also recalls Pollock's splattered canvases, which at least one critic compared to "a flat, war-shattered city, possibly Hiroshima, as seen from a great height."[27] A similar sense of catastrophic aftermath—a forensic motif par excellence—was evoked during the Vietnam War era in works such as Robert Smithson's *Partially Buried Woodshed* (1970), a print of which later Smithson fig. 56 became a memorial poster for the four students shot at Kent State University. In *Defoliation* (1970), Terry Fox's first public performance, the artist Fox fig. 55 employed a type of flamethrower used by the U.S. military in Southeast Asia to burn a rectangular patch of Chinese jasmine in a Berkeley flower garden, bluntly alluding to the Pentagon's "scorched earth" policy in Vietnam.

On the surface *Defoliation* may seem a long way from the concerns of postminimalists like Le Va, yet Fox's work also displays a specific interest in process as well as an aesthetic of aftermath. Only in this case the "stuff lying around the object"—cultural and political issues that were generally excluded from postminimalism—isn't immediately visible.

The trajectory we have followed, in other words, has led from a formalist decentering of the object, in which the surrounding physical context is incorporated into the artwork, to a consideration of the larger social context that frames the making of art. The interest that Le Va and others took in "the absence of specific forms" that characterizes detritus in the studio is also evident in Kienholz's *Illegal Operation*, whose central female figure is so effectively, and

46. Sylvie Fleury; *Sublimes (Chanel Eyeshadow),* 1992; mixed media; dimensions variable; courtesy Postmasters Gallery.

engagingly, horrific precisely because it lacks specific form. This is not to say that the forensic aesthetic inevitably develops toward an explicitly political art, but as we shall see, it does lend itself to exploring matters of public concern.

Traces of Life

To live means to leave traces.
—*Walter Benjamin* [28]

In his essay "Paris, Capital of the Nineteenth Century," Benjamin linked the development of the detective story in the mid-1800s to the evolution of the bourgeois home as a private, enclosed domestic universe. Detective narratives typically revolve around interpreting traces and clues, and these are well preserved indoors: untouched by the elements, blood stains continue to deco- rate a tablecloth, while fingerprints wait patiently on glasses. Evidence of our personal existence, not always available in the theater of public life, reassur- ingly surrounds us in our private dwellings.

In the twentieth century various types of assemblage have utilized domestic artifacts worn with traces of prior life, but these are rarely framed as clues; instead, they typically convey a poetical mythos of the commonplace or a dark romance of impoverishment and mortality. Forensic artworks, by contrast, pre- sent the used object as the record of a singular event or scene. In the late 1950s and early 1960s, for example, Daniel Spoerri created numerous *tableaux pièges* **Spoerri** fig. 12 (snare pictures), wall-mounted tabletops onto which the remains of a meal and place setting had been glued. The composition of these works did not derive from Spoerri's aesthetic decisions, but documented the end result, the final scene, of an actual repast and presented evidence of the artist's bohemian existence.

47. Edward Ruscha, in collaboration with Mason Williams and Patrick Blackwell; *Scene of Strewn Wreckage,* 1967; black-and-white photograph from *Royal Road Test,* 1967 (cat. no. 65).

In a work that directly recalls the *tableaux pièges*, Tom Marioni (under the alias Allan Fish) staged a beer party at the Oakland Museum in 1970 and then exhibited the resulting litter as evidence of prior "sculptural activity."[29] A year later in Los Angeles, Robert Overby entered an abandoned, partially burned house and made latex casts of broken windows, smashed doors, and charred walls. An indexical trace of an actual interior, each work directly reproduced richly textured surfaces, sometimes even including splinters of wood and paint from the original site.

Overby fig. 30, cat. nos. 60–61

All of these works confront the viewer with questions about how we examine the art object itself. Faced with the preserved aftermath of a meal or a damaged section of wall, what should we focus on? Are the haphazardly arranged leftovers somehow meaningful in and of themselves? Or are they primarily significant as the telling sediment of an earlier occurrence?

In the case of Overby's work its ruinous, fragile beauty is clearly haunted by the specter of urban decay, arson, breaking and entering. Though painted to look naturalistic, his skinlike wall sculptures function as environmental fingerprints; dislocated in the gallery's clinical space, they suggest exhibits from a crime lab—a ghostly trace, or negative, of an arena redolent of disorder and violation. Precisely because they indict no one in particular, they conjure an anonymous, lurking destructiveness, an array of asocial behaviors whose motives remain a mystery.

In his Forced Entry photographs of the mid-1970s John Divola bluntly depicted what more clearly seemed to be remnants of criminal activity: violated and damaged homes, marked with graffiti and signs of random destruction. Organized in sequences that suggest an insurance adjustor's methodical surveying practice, these images implicitly linked crime scene photography to the aesthetic of aftermath that characterized then-recent postminimalist practices. Indeed, several pictures feature scattered puddles of broken glass that recall the late-1960s work of Le Va, emphasizing a similarly decentered field of vision.

Divola fig. 29, cat. nos. 23–26

48. Vija Celmins; *Hiroshima*, 1968; graphite on acrylic ground on paper; 13½ x 18 in. (34.3 x 45.7 cm); collection of Leta and Mel Ramos; courtesy McKee Gallery, New York.

At roughly the same time the fingerprint, the forensic trace par excellence, surfaced as a motif in several works by California artists. John Baldessari produced *Art Disaster: Evidence* (1971), a photograph of a broken bowl dusted with lampblack powder, showing four of the artist's fingerprints.[30] Providing a material clue for the solution of a crime—the breaking of a bowl?—it cannily conflates a means of criminal identification with an ironic commentary on the artist's signature "touch."

Baldessari fig. 71, cat. no. 3

Less coy, Bruce Conner's *Prints* (1974), a lockbox containing official correspondence and photocopies of his fingerprints, invoked the potential misuse of bureaucratic power. As the correspondence makes clear, Conner was told that he needed to submit a set of his fingerprints in order to obtain a teaching job at California State University, San Jose (under state policy this had been required of all employees since 1966). He protested that his fingerprints were an integral part of his aesthetic practice. After exchanging a series of letters with college administrators, he finally agreed to produce an edition of them at the Palo Alto police station and then lent a signed copy to Cal State for the duration of his employment.

Conner fig. 33, cat. no. 21

Besides calling attention to the state's possible violation of his civil rights, Conner's work evokes a history of police documentation that relies on bodily traces. Playing off that history, David Hammons's *Admissions Office*, made in 1969, presents a black body print inked onto an office door. Unlike Nauman's earlier work in which he pressed his flesh against a glass pane, Hammons's print has a distinct social context. The faceless body that seems to have slammed into the door, as if denied entrance, stands as rhetorical evidence of the "closed-door" policy toward African-Americans practiced by many American colleges and other mainstream institutions.

Hammons fig. 24, cat. no. 33

Burden's *Sculpture in Three Parts* (1974) also employed a trace of the artist's body to conjure a type of crime scene, although the victim in this case

Burden fig. 34, cat. no. 18

49. Bruce Nauman; *Composite Photo of Two Messes on the Studio Floor*, 1967; gelatin-silver print; 40½ x 123 in. (102.9 x 312.4 cm); The Museum of Modern Art, New York, gift of Philip Johnson. Photograph ©1996 The Museum of Modern Art, New York.

was not a social group so much as an idea of art. At the Hansen Fuller Gallery in San Francisco Burden sat on a metal stool placed atop a plinth, attended by a succession of photographers; after forty-three hours he finally fell to the ground, an event captured by one of his personal paparazzi. A chalk outline of his body's position on the floor was then exhibited alongside the unoccupied plinth and chair. Besides testifying to a feat of endurance, these ghostly artifacts were posed as polemical evidence that a certain conception of art and of the artist's role had been knocked off its pedestal. As the trace of a physical action, Burden's piece harked back directly to Pollock, yet the chalk outline, suggestive of those used to record the position of a body at the scene of a crime or accident, added an ominous note. It seemed to imply that once the art object was linked to the artist's prior physical process, it became inextricably entangled with his mortality and so was banished from the timeless platform of traditional art.[31]

Revisiting this scene, Jeffrey Vallance's *Run Over Art Shipment* (1990) consists of a piece of actual evidence: a damaged shipping package containing original drawings by the artist. Several accompanying letters from an insurance adjustor inform us that the package was run over by a moving company that had been hired to return Vallance's unsold art from a New York gallery (its surface is in fact conspicuously marked by a large tire tread). Redefined as the physical record of an accident, the work is inextricably linked to a destructive history; in place of the art object's immortal status, it betrays a pathetic transience and highlights the vulnerability of artistic identity in the face of institutional forces.

Vallance cat. no. 70

In the late 1980s and early 1990s Anthony Hernandez explored a different kind of poignant transience in his Landscapes for the Homeless series, color photographs of improvised encampments throughout Los Angeles. Usually devoid of human figures, these images depict the belongings and refuse of those forced to

Hernandez fig. 22, cat. nos. 38–40

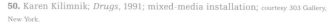

50. Karen Kilimnik; *Drugs*, 1991; mixed-media installation; courtesy 303 Gallery, New York.

make their "homes" under freeway overpasses and in overgrown urban lots. On one level these pictures indirectly recall reconnaissance photos; their disordered scenes suggest places abandoned in a hurry, perhaps only moments before a police sweep. Their lingering, understated power derives in part from this aura of recent departure and the eerie sense of loss that accompanies it. Hernandez has thus forged a cogent means of portraying people trapped in a marginalized existence: represented only by the fugitive non-sites they inhabit, their "invisible" lives are left for the viewer to piece together, using the evidence from what appears to be the scene of a vast and endlessly recurring crime.

Staged Evidence

For the detective, nothing is ever truly itself and nothing more.

—*Philip Kerr* [32]

The theatricality of evidence is demonstrated in our courtrooms on a regular basis; in the hands of a histrionic prosecutor the bloody baseball bat becomes a prop in a dramatic performance. Yet there is a stagy quality to evidence even before it is produced in court, which derives in part from its double identity: the bloody baseball bat is at once a commonplace object and an uncanny incarnation of evil.

This curious mechanism, by which an artifact's meaning is uncannily doubled, is a familiar one in the art world, where for much of this century found objects have been reframed to take on meanings that have little to do with their everyday use. Yet, unlike the surrealist object, which conforms to fairly specific poetic parameters, evidence reveals this semantic shift at its most arbitrary, a fact played on by Baldessari's *Free Rolling Tire* (1971–72). One of his   **Baldessari** cat. no. 4

51. Joseph Beuys, *Terremoto in Palazzo*, 1981; mixed-media installation; collection Fondazione Amelio.

52. US Air flight 427 wreckage at airport hangar in Pittsburgh. ©Pittsburgh Post-Gazette. Reprinted with permission.

first works to use violence as a motif, it juxtaposes five snapshots of a rolling tire with a newspaper clipping about a fatal collision between a free-rolling truck tire and a pedestrian. We are left to ponder whether the tire in the snapshots is a potential agent of death or a harmless object; its definition, as Baldessari wryly implies, cannot be based on "inherent" characteristics, but instead is contingent on how it "behaves."

Ripe with revelatory potential, the scene of an accident or crime is thus a place where every detail, no matter how mundane, is a potential hub of meaning. Terry Allen's *Memory House* (1973) economically evokes this delirious circumstance: to a found black-and-white photograph of an empty living room, Allen added tags of paper marking different times of day, as if charting the course of a criminal act. Although it resembles a police lab document, the photo serves only as a magnet for possible readings. As one writer observed, it leaves us with "a surfeit of evidence allowing no interpretation except what we might find in our own memory."[33]

Allen fig. 35, cat. no. 1

Alexis Smith probed a similar idea in *All the Simple Old Fashioned Charm* (1984), a wooden school chair whose appearance in the gallery initially suggests a prop without a stage—at least until we read the hard-boiled phrase written on its seat: "All the simple old-fashioned charm of a cop beating up a drunk." In light of this text the chair becomes a prop around which we mentally reconstruct a brutal encounter; its worn and scuffed surface is metaphorically transformed into a surrogate for a victim's bruised flesh. Smith's stolen phrase co-opts the object's "real" history, evident in its surface markings, and attaches it to a pulp-fiction memory.

Smith fig. 25, cat. no. 67

We have already seen how the same artifact—whether a tire or a performance relic—can appear at once to be utterly mundane and yet charged with a surplus meaning that eludes our visual inspection and so seems vaguely uncanny. As Philip Kerr has observed, to the detective "a cigarette end was never just a cigarette end: it was also sometimes a sign, a clue, a piece in a puzzle awaiting connection with something else."[34] We may learn about a thing's meaning, in other words, only by understanding its place in a larger symbolic structure. Consideration of the crime scene leads us, in this way, to a "postmodern" understanding in which the same object can shift between opposing categories, functioning "successively as a disgusting reject and as a sublime, charismatic apparition."[35] Such is the case with Mike Kelley's *Yarn #3* (1990), a tangle of black, white, and yellow yarn on a white blanket. The viewer encounters what appears to be a pathetic aftermath, an entropic residue, yet the yarn also evokes Pollock's sublime skeins of splattered paint, while its placement on the floor wryly recalls the artist's working method and the horizontal drift to which his imagery ultimately returns us.

Kelley fig. 72, cat. no. 42

Where does one find the meaning of such a work? The unstructured aspect of *Yarn #3* works against the gallery's geometrically hygienic and vertically oriented frame. It is a matter not of the walls "donating their content" to the object, as O'Doherty suggested, but of a meaning or value created through a specific relationship. An object is thus neither sublime nor pathetic in and of itself, as we can access its meaning only by considering its place in a larger system.

This detachment of meaning from the individual image or object contributes to the aura of theatricality hovering over forensic art. It may be helpful, in this context, to recall Michael Fried's definition of "theatricality" in his famous diatribe against minimalism. Fried claimed that such work was theatrical because, rather than drawing spectators into contemplating its internal dynamics, it stressed an "objective," external relationship to the viewer. Such art required active participation; indeed, the viewer's experience constituted the work's actual content. "Theatricality" was thus the product of an aesthetic in which art, as Fried argued, was reduced to being a mere object in need of an investigation.[36]

What Fried lamented, essentially, was the loss of a "self-contained" object, yet, as noted above, all evidence taunts us with a theatrical double identity. This is clear even in Janet Fries's black-and-white images of San Francisco homicide sites, taken in 1975. Access to murder sites is typically limited to homicide detectives and the coroner's crew, and while this is obviously a precaution against contamination, it also shrouds the scene in a kind of aesthetic parentheses. By carefully framing the ritually sealed-off space of official investigation, Fries's photographs investigate a set of circumstances in which reality takes on the quality of a staged tableau.

Fries figs. 20, 38; cat. nos. 31–32

Mike Mandel and Larry Sultan's *Evidence* (1977)—a collection of black-and-white photographs from the archives of police and fire departments, insurance underwriters' laboratories, aircraft manufacturers, and scientific testing firms—explores this curious theatricality from another tangent. Most of the found images in *Evidence* depict scenes of aftermath: craters made by explosions, burn marks, materials left over from various testing procedures, including "accidents" that appear to have been deliberately staged. The contrast between their set-up quality and the "chaos" they scrupulously record lends them a deadpan absurdity. They seem disconcertingly "unreal" and resist our attempts to definitively contain or locate them.

Mandel, Sultan fig. 73, cat. no. 51

54. Jeff Wall; *The Destroyed Room*, 1978; Cibachrome transparency; 62½ x 19¼ in. (159 x 48.9 cm); courtesy Marian Goodman Gallery, New York.

Many of Kienholz's pioneering walk-in environments evince a similarly uneasy mix of the "real" and theatrical; indeed, the artist acknowledged that he thought of a life-size installation such as *Five Car Stud* (1969–72), which utilized real automobiles, as "a stage set for a play."[37] *White Easel with Machine Pistol* (1975)—which Kienholz made with his wife, Nancy Reddin Kienholz—presents what appears to be an unfinished sculpture temporarily abandoned in the studio by its creators. Paraphernalia of artistic production— sheets of galvanized metal, a machine pistol, and work light—are placed around a model of a wood-beam easel from the Kienholzes' Idaho workshop. While the machine pistol quietly recalls the themes of violence that recur throughout their oeuvre, what is foregrounded here is a sense of desolate absence, like that haunting a stage set at intermission.

Kienholz fig. 74, cat. no. 44

By presenting a site of interrupted activity, *White Easel* points to the constructed and provisional aspect of the art object. It counsels us that the installation before us, as Kabakov has stated of his own work, "is deceit and that everything has been made 'intentionally,' specially, in order to create an impression."[38] We are here enjoined not to interpret the tableau in literal terms (a fate that the Kienholzes' work suffers all too often), but to reconstruct the aesthetic process, the heterogeneous chain of decisions through which forms come to take on cluelike meanings.

Paul McCarthy's *Bossy Burger* (1993) accents this dialogue between absence and presence by incorporating the "original" event into the installation. Next to a stage set from a discontinued family sitcom, despoiled by traces of prior mayhem (pieces of rotting meat, emptied condiment bottles, stained furniture), two monitors play an hour-long videotape showing the artist, dressed in a chef's outfit and Alfred E. Neuman mask, conducting a deranged cooking and drawing lesson and obsessively probing the architectural boundaries of the homey set.

McCarthy fig. 14

In *Bossy Burger* the absent event is made tantalizingly available through video. Like Vito Acconci's *Seedbed*, a 1972 performance in which the artist lay under a false floor in a gallery, masturbating and taunting "spectators" who could not see him, McCarthy's installation replaces the confrontation of live performance with the alienated seduction of a removed one. Yet it is this missing third term—the live performer—that ultimately haunts our encounter with the work. Sounds from the continuously playing videotape lend the physical environment a ghostly aspect, as if a traumatized spirit still prowled its confines. We are left to ponder a realm of "live" experience to which we have no direct access but can know only through different types of traces, all framed by theatrical artifice.

Acconci fig. 106

Sam Durant's Abandoned Houses (1995), maquettes of trashed Case Study houses, confront the viewer with a miniature theater of desecration. These deserted dream homes, remnants of a modernist utopia where the well-designed house was a prop for a model existence, are littered with debris and overturned furniture; walls and ceilings are punctured by gaping holes or splashed with graffiti. Such signs of disorder and vandalism invoke social forces unaccounted for by the narrow idealism and spiritual hygiene of modernist architecture. Because of their scale, however, Durant's maquettes

Durant fig. 19, cat. no. 28

convey only a theoretical possibility. They thus conflate the uncanny allure of miniatures, which typically present an empty world waiting to be imaginatively inhabited by the spectator, with the dry factuality of courtroom exhibits such as the dollhouse models of homicide scenes made by Frances Glessner Lee in the 1940s.

Lee figs. 5, 6

Kozloff described postminimalist sculpture as symbolizing "an action process, *about to be commenced*, or already completed" (italics added), and likewise the forensic aesthetic is not limited to objects or scenes that bear the imprint of prior activities. Nayland Blake's S&M-equipped stainless-steel "workstations" from the late 1980s appear curiously immaculate. They conjure spectacles yet to be enacted, rituals of eroticized punishment and restraint, or perhaps those of institutional medical care and "official" torture. Even as they invite us to become performers, these theatrically clinical sculptures appear spooked by the ghosts of their (presumably) intended users, absent bodies that remain forever offstage.

Blake fig. 104, cat. no. 11

Bodies of Evidence

Art exists in a kind of eternity of display and ... [this] gives the gallery a limbolike status; one has to have died already to be there.
—*Brian O'Doherty* [39]

Not long after the notion of "action art" began to proliferate in various forms, the body itself was displayed in the gallery as a symbolic object. In 1959 James Lee Byars presented himself, sitting alone in the middle of a room, as the only "artwork" in an exhibition. The notion that Byars's physical presence constituted an aesthetic product could be seen as an extension of the

55. Terry Fox; *Defoliation*, 1970; photograph of a performance at the University Art Museum, Berkeley; courtesy Reese Palley Gallery, San Francisco.

abstract expressionists' belief that the artwork directly reflected the artist's unique self. Yet it seems more than mere coincidence that the body was introduced as artistic evidence at almost the very moment that the traditional art object vanished.

What had vanished, of course, was not the production of art but a set of ideas about its cultural status. While critics like Rosenberg bewailed the dispersal or dissipation of modernist aesthetics into the mass marketplace,[40] others fretted over the effects of the art world's own commercialization and the increasing influence of the international art trade. Under such circumstances the artist could no longer pose as an autonomous creator; as Marcel Duchamp caustically pointed out, "With commercialization has come the integration of the artist into society, for the first time in a hundred years. . . . Today the artist is integrated, and so he has to be paid, and so he has to keep producing for the market."[41]

Thus, at the very moment when art's status began to seem that of a weightless commodity circulating in a network of spectacle, the body itself arrived on the scene as sculptural material—not just the body but its waste products as well. In 1961 Piero Manzoni ingeniously offered both his canned excrement and bottled breath for sale as works of art. These souvenirs mocked the modern artist's recently acquired role of celebrity, but, more importantly, they conjured the artist's irretrievably alienated status in postwar Europe's accelerated culture of consumption. As Benjamin Buchloh has observed, Manzoni's strategic response was to "withdraw altogether the pictorial and sculptural signifiers so dear to fashion and design and to replace them with the last site of resistance, the body's actual materialities, blood, breath, and excrement"—pieces of physical evidence that could not be easily transformed into spectacular displays.[42]

Just as the forensic pathologist is accustomed to thinking of the corpse not as a coherent whole but as a site of prior actions, a collection of parts that

56. Robert Smithson; *Partially Buried Woodshed*, 1970; one woodshed, twenty truckloads of dirt; estate of Robert Smithson; courtesy John Weber Gallery.

57. Abigail Lane; *Incident Room*, 1993; wax body, human hair; dimensions variable; courtesy Glenn Scott Wright Contemporary Art, London.

tell a story, recent examples of forensic art similarly address the body as a dispersed territory of clues and traces. For *The Artifact Piece* (1986) James Luna displayed his own body in precisely such terms at San Diego's Museum of Man. In a gallery dedicated to the Kumeyaay tribe, which resided in San Diego County, he lay face-up on a sand-covered table, wearing only a "traditional" loincloth; to the casual observer he appeared to be a stuffed exhibit. In contrast to Byars's existential self-presentation, Luna exhibited himself as an object attached to a specific cultural history. The various scars on his body, which accompanying texts attributed to the drunken brawls that mark life on contemporary reservations, portrayed an unsentimental view of Indian life, yet as a "live" artifact, Luna's body offered crucial evidence contradicting the museum's portrait of Indian culture as something purely historic.

Richard Misrach's Playboy series (1989–91) consists of magazine images that have been perforated and ripped into fragments by gunfire. (Misrach found the magazines at a Nevada shooting range.) The *Playboy* cover models were presumably the intended targets, but bullets blindly penetrated interior images and advertisements as well. Reproduced at a large scale, these shot-up magazine pages viscerally underscore the parallel between the forensic and the pornographic gaze, each of which isolates its object from its context in time and space. Misrach's clinical approach self-consciously mirrors that of his subject—magazines that portray bodies as inanimate targets for sexual firing practice.

Monica Majoli's small oil paintings of scarred flesh also suggest forensic photographs, only as if reworked in the style of Northern Renaissance art. Closely cropped body parts reveal lines presumably left by sharp instruments; a section of pelvis or a wrist and forearm, for example, are traversed by thin red scars. Though imbued with quasi-religious eroticism by Majoli's Old Master technique, the fragment of flesh is significant mainly as a recording surface, not unlike the ground of a painting. The close-up framing further imparts an almost autobiographical intimacy to the images, leaving us to wonder if these might be portraits of self-inflicted wounds on the artist's body.

In *Autopsy* (1994), a videotape by Bob Flanagan and Sheree Rose, the body likewise appears as a recording surface. Throughout the tape Flanagan lies naked and seemingly unconscious on a gurney, a thin, pale figure seemingly prepared for the coroner's probing eye and hand. With the air of someone conducting an informal medical class, Rose intimately revisits her partner's various body parts while verbally recollecting—and physically reenacting—their sadomasochistic rituals. In the process she reconstrues his flesh as a map of impressions made by external objects and actions, each linked to a specific past.

In the Prague police museum an exhibit devoted to a local serial killer includes a display of the suitcases in which he carried his victims' hacked-up remains. Evoking this kind of eerie relic of dismemberment, Michelle Rollman's untitled assemblage of 1995 presents a torsolike pillow, wrapped in a medical corset and displayed in a velvet-lined case as if it were the fetishized remnant

Luna fig. 94

Misrach fig. 77, cat. nos. 54–55

Majoli fig. 78, cat. nos. 49–50

Flanagan, Rose fig. 79, cat. no. 30

Rollman fig. 80, cat. no. 63

58. Anthony Hernandez; *Shooting Sites (Angeles National Forest #1)*, 1988 (cat. no. 37).

of a corpse. A cutout news photo and manically scrawled writing add to the impression of a creepily obsessive shrine. The text's repeated references to "fat" hint that the mechanism of fetishization here is related to the idealized standards of beauty by which women's bodies are often judged in our culture—a necrophilic aesthetic in that it reduces persons to the status of inanimate objects.

This logic of fragmentation reaches a climax of sorts in Richard Hawkins's *Poison* (1991), a rubber mask that has been carefully peeled into strips, which droop from the wall like a tangle of shredded skin. Adorned with photos of male fanzine idols, *Poison* suggests a prop left over from a fetishistic performance—tales of serial killers who skin their victims come to mind. Like the handiwork of an obsessive fan, it provokes us to speculate about the motivations behind its making—the ratio of sexual desire, frustration, and rage it seemingly embodies in its splintered flesh.

Hawkins fig. 81, cat. no. 36

In George Stone's installation *Unknown, Unwanted, Unconscious, Untitled* (1993), bodies appear to be whole but are hidden from view. Inside latex body bags articulated robotic skeletons perform lifelike movements. Scattered across the gallery floor, they recall the "bag people" whose bodies often litter the streets of cities like anonymous corpses. This work thus intimately engages us with the scene of a collective crime in which almost every museum visitor is implicated: not the fact of homelessness, but the social invisibility of the homeless.

Stone fig. 82, cat. no. 68

We can also regard Stone's installation as a desublimation of minimalist sculpture. By implanting signs of life in minimalism's hollow, anthropomorphically scaled rectangles, he makes plain what such reductivist art elided: signs of the body's fragility and the social context that frames it. This is one of the virtues of the forensic approach: it inevitably returns us to the larger scene and allows a reading in which formal and social issues are not at odds but can be considered compatible clues.

The Framing Absence

A clue in the detective sense may be of an intangible as well as a tangible nature; it may derive from the absence of a relevant object as well as from the presence of an irrelevant one.
—*William O'Green* [43]

With the epic sweep of history painting, Lewis Baltz's *11777 Foothill Boulevard, Los Angeles, CA* (1991) portrays a bland strip of Southern California-style urban blight, a generic Los Angeles streetscape of the kind that can be easily overlooked because it offers no immediate reason to examine it more carefully. But the photo's monumental scale amplifies the landscape's impersonal banality to a point where it no longer seems so innocent. As an art critic for the *Los Angeles Times* observed, the picture seems to chronicle an "urban void in which nothing good can thrive." [44]

Baltz fig. 23, cat. no. 7

In fact, Baltz's image depicts not just any "urban void" but the scene of one of the most publicized crimes in recent memory: the 1991 beating of Rodney King by officers of the Los Angeles Police Department. For those with a memory for significant addresses, the title is a giveaway; otherwise, Baltz's photo seems to withhold as much information as it reveals. Refusing to "spill the beans," it forces us to reexamine the mundane clues before us as traces of the social and economic forces that have produced such a blighted environment.

Baltz's use of a horizontal format is an ironic device: the photo's breadth promises to show us everything, to ensure that no detail is left out, yet it is ultimately concerned with meanings that lie beyond its (visual) boundaries. Photographs in general, as Roland Barthes eloquently argued,[45] are haunted by absence and loss; each confronts us with the trace of an irretrievably vanished human moment. But the absence in question here is of a different order; it is a framing absence.

Any good investigator, of course, must have a nose for such situations, for smelling out the significance not only of seemingly trivial clues but of non-events and missing details as well. Sherlock Holmes's typical advice to Watson that he contemplate the overall gestalt of the crime scene, rather than focusing on specific aspects, implies that clues do not betray their secrets when directly examined; their story emerges only if they are approached obliquely. The forensic aesthetic, in this way, accepts a certain alienation as a precondition of meaning—and even finds in it some positive value.

This discussion sets the picture, so to speak, for Uta Barth's Ground series. **Barth** fig. 21, Each photo conveys the impression that Barth had focused on a sitter who cat. nos. 8–10 departed before the shutter was snapped, leaving only a blurred background for the camera to record. Devoid of apparent subject, these images provoke us to scrutinize mechanisms of composition and lighting and to examine the usually overlooked backdrops used to set off, or subtly inflect, a sitter's "character." But

59. Duane Hanson; *War (Vietnam Scene)*, 1960; polyester resin, fiberglass, mixed media; dimensions variable; courtesy Mrs. Duane Hanson.

it is the camera's unsettlingly soft focus, its missing clarity, that is the most critical absence here. It strands us on ambiguous ground; we can no longer be sure that there is not somehow something more to these preternaturally calm interiors. This uncertainty sparks a kind of paranoia; every hazy detail before us seems to hint at concealed significance. The absence of visual clarity thus transforms the photo's content into something suspicious, opening a void into which we plunge like obsessive investigators, compulsively producing interpretations.

At first Sharon Lockhart's untitled image of 1996 seems to invite a different kind of fall: its impressive cliff and seascape evinces an undertone of inexplicable menace, as if it were the scene of a deadly accident or the site of a planned one. Yet when we examine it more closely, Lockhart's image appears suspect. Because the camera's acute perspective flattens the depicted space, we find ourselves faced with an uncertain space where even falling becomes problematic. This missing frisson of vertigo is itself a clue, a warning that the picture is not what it appears to be. Its apparent "reality" derives not from the image's documentary function but from its familiarity; it calls to mind an ominous shot from a Hitchcock movie or a setting in a Caspar David Friedrich painting. Charged with our media-filtered memories, Lockhart's photo seems to radiate an excess of "reality," which in this case may make us anxious as we sense that there is more here than meets the eye.

Lockhart fig. 83, cat. no. 47

Nancy Reese's heroically scaled *El Señor* (1990), an oil painting of a ship burning at sea, initially appears to belong to a familiar genre of nautical pictures, namely, the disaster at sea, in which nature's powers are displayed in a sublime inferno of water and fire. Yet Reese's pictorial rhetoric subtly mixes Old Master flourishes with modernist and cinematic tropes, so that the ghostly scene, when closely examined, reveals itself as a work of bricolage. The intent behind the image meanwhile seems to oscillate between divergent impulses: the allegorical, on the one hand, and "straight" representation, on the other.

Reese fig. 84, cat. no. 62

60. Guerilla Art Action Group; *Blood Bath (A Call for the Immediate Resignation of All the Rockefellers from the Board of Trustees of the Museum of Modern Art);* performance at the Museum of Modern Art, New York, November 18, 1969.

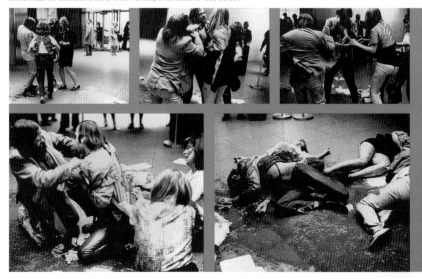

Instead of a unified reality, the picture lures us into a series of traps and hidden ruses in which visual information seems contaminated or, at the very least, unstable.

Because Reese leaves us no clear cues as to how we should interpret the "evidence" before us, any attempt to penetrate this suspicious appearance is doomed. We must simply make note of it, proceeding like the seasoned investigator who accepts that there is no realm of uncompromised data where the truth lies unsullied. Unlike the "Just the facts, Ma'am" detective of pulp fiction, such an investigator is under no illusion that his task involves dealing with objective "facts" per se, so much as with nuance and ambiguity.

Luna's *Tribal Identity* (1995) demands a similar approach from the audience. It presents paired before-and-after photos that summon a missing history. The first set juxtaposes an official portrait of turn-of-the-century Apache youths wearing traditional dress with a group portrait as they appeared a year later, groomed and attired in Western fashion after having attended a federal boarding school. The second pair contrasts recent photos of Indian students: in the "before" shot they seemingly epitomize preppy fashion, while in the "after" shot—taken after they had spent time at school—they appear in "militant" pan-Indian costume.

Luna fig. 76,
cat. no. 48

Each set of pictures leaves us with an enigma: what has occurred off-screen, as it were, to produce such dramatic changes in appearance? The earlier photos, one might reasonably suspect, were taken to promote the benefits of an education that could transform wild Indian youths into model Americans. The second set is clearly ironic, however; the students' tribal demeanor in the "after" photo appears as artificial as the makeover in the earlier pictures. While we cannot tear away this "false" veil to reveal their "true" identities, we can discern the intention behind it; namely, to impress upon the world their authentic Native American status. The context

61. Yves Klein; *Anthropométries de l'époque bleue (Anthropometries of the Blue Period)*, 1960; performance at Galerie Internationale d'Art Contemporain, Paris, March 9, 1960.

of this work then becomes clearer: for cultural police seeking to locate the "real Indian," Luna's installation presents an unsolvable mystery—an identity that seems suspect even as it embraces the traditional.

In Eileen Cowin's untitled photograph of 1997 an empty tub draped with green fabric eerily recalls one of art history's most famous crime scenes: Jacques-Louis David's *Death of Marat* (1793), a neoclassical rendering of the assassinated revolutionary hero. In Cowin's photograph the dramatically lit tableau floats in theatrical space, calling to mind a backdrop from a portrait studio. Yet the original subject is conspicuously missing. In the corpse's absence the empty bathtub seems to reserve a space for the viewer, beckoning us to take our place in history. Since our presence is forever inscribed outside the picture plane, the scene's import is relegated to a state of suspense, and we are left with a view into history's contingent construction, its incomplete character appearing "objective" thanks only to our identification.

Cowin fig. 85,
cat. no. 22

David fig. 95

Bodies are conspicuously absent as well from John Divola's *Broken Furniture and Evidence of Aggression* (1995), a collection of twelve continuity stills from Warner Bros. crime films of the 1930s. In contrast to lively scenes of celluloid violence, these deadpan images permit prolonged contemplation of a type of disordered still life—domestic sets replete with overturned furniture, broken china, skewed picture frames. Continuity stills are used to facilitate precise re-creation of a given set should a sequence require additional shots at a later date, and as such, these photographs evince a clear forensic intention. This documentary veneer can be misleading, however: smashed chair legs and other indications of "violence" are not actually evidence of the offstage actors' prior behavior but are carefully manufactured props, and the scene we behold is a newly created ruin. The slate bearing the name of the film and its director which appears in the lower corner of most of these images is not the only giveaway. The even studio lighting, too-precise decoration, and sterile, generic atmosphere also clue us in that these disordered interiors are in fact carefully arranged. Just as a detective may perceive "the very absence of a trace as itself a trace," so does the telltale absence of imperfection serve here as an indelible mark of artifice.[46]

Divola fig. 3,
cat. no. 27

Beyond Suspicion

The genius of suspicion has come into the world.
—*Stendhal*[47]

In 1981 French artist Sophie Calle had her mother hire a private detective, with instructions to take surveillance photos of Calle as she wandered around Paris. As the artist was unaware of her stalker's identity, *La Filature* (The shadow, 1981) engages our collective fascination with the stranger, among other things.[48] This cultural preoccupation tellingly manifests itself in the popular obsession with serial killers. Whereas the mystery story reassures us that a thorough investigation will always uncover the truth about our fellow citizens,

Calle fig. 98

the serial killer—at least when he proves to be the perfectly nice gentleman next door—subverts such belief, raising the suspicion that we do not, perhaps even *cannot*, really know the truth about our neighbors. This figure conjures more radical possibilities as well: namely, that each self harbors unsuspected, and undetectable, dimensions and that identity may prove to be far more baroque than we had imagined, involving subterranean circuits of desire that leave no visible clues.

It is not only our neighbors who are strangers; it turns out that we may not actually know ourselves. How can we be sure, then, that we are not, like Oedipus Rex, the very criminal whose trail we are investigating? With stunning bluntness, Kienholz's *Sawdy* (1971) poses precisely this question. On the stained window of a Datsun pickup door, Kienholz silkscreened a black-and-white image of his *Five Car Stud*, a nightmarish lynching scene set in a parking lot. Surrounded by a circle of cars, a group of monstrous white men are shown castrating an African-American, while a white woman seated alone in a pickup truck appears to be vomiting in anguish. These elements alone provide enough information for us to reconstruct the events leading up to the crime we behold, but *Sawdy* is also concerned with the absent gaze that frames this scene.

Kienholz cat. no. 43

By placing us in a roadside seat, *Sawdy* inescapably implicates each viewer as both witness and indifferent voyeur. It is the second role, however, that Kienholz stresses: to actually see the image of *Five Car Stud*, the viewer must first roll down a concealing pane of mirrored glass. As one image displaces the other, our own reflection is intimately linked with the scene of the crime. The absent subject in this tableau of racist violence, the missing figure that haunts it, is the specter of the audience's voyeurism.

Twenty years after Kienholz made this artwork, it was uncannily echoed by the relentlessly televised footage of LAPD officers beating Rodney King. Through the mass media we routinely become voyeurs of such crime scenes,

62. Saburo Murakami; *Work Painted by Throwing a Ball*, 1954; rubber ball soaked in watercolor paint, thrown onto paper; 41⅞ x 29¾ in. (105.8 x 75.6 cm); courtesy Ashiya City Museum of Art and History.

and as Kienholz seemed to acknowledge, our experience of violence is then primarily an aesthetic one. "Only the victim knows the brutal 'reality'" of criminal assault, as Joel Black points out. "The rest of us view it at a distance, often as rapt onlookers."[49]

In a moralistic society the thrill of witnessing a criminal act is construed as something shameful. In "On Murder Considered as One of the Fine Arts," De Quincey quotes Lactantius, an early Christian writer, to the effect that "merely to be present at a murder fastens on a man the character of an accomplice; barely to be a spectator involves us in one common guilt with the perpetrator."[50] It is as if by simply watching a violent assault, whether committed by law officer or criminal, we become identified with the perpetrator's actions so that they seem to enact our own secret impulses.

In Vincent Fecteau's installation *Ben* (1994) the spectator is likewise ensnared. A group of shoe box constructions lie on the floor, evoking low-tech rat traps with a slight modernist flair. Cat's heads gaze down from a photocollage on the wall with glistening eyes, as if waiting for a potential victim to emerge. Apart from this narrative element, the shoe boxes' provisional, almost speculative demeanor suggests cheap scale models, architectural layouts for as-yet-unrealized works. Faced with constructions that in turn conjure absent objects, we find ourselves caught in a trap where the "real" eludes us.

Fecteau's titles provide teasing clues, however: *Ben*, as fans of animal-revenge films will no doubt remember, was the title of a movie about a boy's pet rat, featuring an eponymous theme song sung by pop superstar Michael Jackson. The title *Shirley Temple Room #8* (1994) should ring a bell for those with a memory for scandal, as it was the name of the room where Jackson entertained young boys at his "Never-Never Land" ranch, including the child whose family brought sexual molestation charges against the singer.

Fecteau fig. 86, cat. no. 29

Beyond alluding to a mediascape where every hero is suspect and even "Never-Never Land" can be reconstrued as a crime scene, Fecteau's installation also raises questions about the viewer's involvement, though far less bluntly than Kienholz's *Sawdy*. If Jackson's legendary consumption of cuteness—his fixation on Disneyland and Peter Pan—was a cover for less innocent desires, then what of our own cultural consumption of cuteness—of cat foldouts in pet magazines, of child stars like Shirley Temple, or of Jackson himself, for that matter? And what of the voyeuristic pleasure we take in a star's lurid downfall, not to mention our vicarious enjoyment of his supposed sexual transgressions?

We are indirectly reminded here that on one level the crime scene functions as a hub of pleasure. The criminal act itself is frequently experienced as a moment of ecstatic excitement, as Jack Katz persuasively documents in his book *Seductions of Crime*.[51] In this light the crime scene appears as a kind of postorgasmic landscape, a monument to a delirious, fugitive joy.

D-L Alvarez's *The Boomin System (Hold On I'm Coming)* (1995), inspired by an actual curbside memorial to the victim of a drive-by shooting, discreetly alludes to this illicit delight. A row of unlabeled forty-ounce beer bottles sit on the floor in front of a collection of magazine photos that hang on the wall. A lowly memorial in every sense, it calls to mind the aftermath of a

Alvarez fig. 87, cat. no. 2

63. Lucio Fontana; *Concetto spaziale, Attese*, 1967–68; red painting on canvas; 25½ x 21¼ in. (65 x 54 cm); courtesy Barbara Gladstone Gallery.

drunken party. We can view the magazine clippings, a mix of imagery evoking desire and sentimentality, only through the bottles' yellow liquids, so that they look blurred and hazy, as if we ourselves were "under the influence" or were reexperiencing the murderer's intoxication. A nearby boom box plays a tape of street noises (recorded at the scene of the drive-by) in which Fourth of July firecrackers and backfiring cars sound like random gunfire.

Besides referring to the delirious excitement of crime, *The Boomin System* reminds us that the crime scene is not only a scene of investigation but also a site of mourning. Indeed, the most celebrated icon of crime in Western art history—the Crucifixion—has traditionally been framed in just these terms. Disaster has its dark allure, but our response as witnesses is plainly not limited to schadenfreude or simple fascination.

Elaborating on this idea, Lyle Ashton Harris's investigatory installation *The Watering Hole* (1996) takes as its starting point our fascination with Jeffrey **Harris** fig. 89, cat. nos. 34–35 Dahmer, the serial killer who lured teenage males, mainly African- and Asian-Americans, to a Milwaukee apartment, where he murdered them and then, in some cases, committed acts of necrophilia and cannibalism. Harris's large photographic panels depict an assortment of images and texts pinned and stenciled onto wood paneling. Shot through blood-red filters with the unforgiving light of police photographs, the collected magazine covers, news clippings, and personal correspondence assume the status of documentary evidence. Indeed, their composition calls to mind a detective's "case progress board," where clues are showcased not only to chart an investigation's development but also (hopefully) to jar the viewer into realizing some as-yet-unseen connection among disparate bits of information.

Sifting through Harris's homemade data bank, one finds repeated references to Dahmer and his victims, as well as images of African-American sports stars and models. In a sense these images present evidence of a *conceptual* investigation,

64. Yoko Ono; *Smoke Painting*, 1961; canvas and sumi ink; 30 x 42 in. (76.2 x 106.7 cm) approx.; exhibited at AG Gallery, New York, summer 1961; present whereabouts unknown.

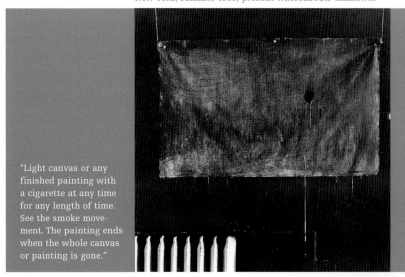

"Light canvas or any finished painting with a cigarette at any time for any length of time. See the smoke movement. The painting ends when the whole canvas or painting is gone."

allowing us to reconstitute the artist's thought processes as he pondered links between Dahmer's crimes and the larger "scene" surrounding them: a society in which the black male body has been fetishized and gay desire coyly commodified in fashion and advertising. Deliberately withholding any neat solutions, Harris's work leaves us with the suspicion that Dahmer's desires were less a cultural aberration than a "watering hole" in our national psyche, from which we all drink.

Criminal Guarantees

This is the essence of crime: if it is perfect, it leaves no clue, no trace. So what guarantees the world's existence for us is its accidental, criminal, imperfect character.
—*Jean Baudrillard* [52]

Since the late nineteenth century the forensic sciences have offered assurance that the truth of any given event is knowable after the fact, that our unseen deeds can be traced and accounted for by the forces of law and order. In a sense the forensic lab took on the absolute authority of a divinity; it was God, after all, who previously guaranteed the veracity of history by witnessing our every act and secret trespass. But our modernist faith in science ushered in the belief that the parameters of the real are comprehensible in their smallest detail and that we do indeed possess objective forms of knowledge.

The forensic *aesthetic,* by contrast, stresses the contingency of any given viewpoint. In this respect it parallels a wide spectrum of "postmodern" experience, which is distinguished in no small part by our decaying belief in the reality of clear and separable things-in-themselves, whether "truth" or the psychological monad of the self. Doubt, not belief, characterizes our present age. Perhaps it is no wonder, then, that criminal proceedings have

65. Niki de Saint Phalle at a shooting session in Malibu, California, March 4, 1962.

become a national entertainment: we are fascinated by the drama of the jury—our surrogates—in judging which voices to trust among the procession of witnesses and competing experts that make up a trial. And as followers of Court TV are well aware, the forensic laboratory is no longer seen as a repository of truth; its evidence can be thrown into doubt by skilled attorneys who cast suspicion on the competency of technicians or, by attributing ulterior motives to a "neutral" official agency, the findings of science.

This kind of pervasive doubt, which insists that truth is always relative, is distinctly different from the suspiciousness that characterizes modernist thought. From the urban paranoia noted by Benjamin in his comments on Atget ("Is not every spot of our cities the scene of a crime?") to philosophical systems such as Marxism and psychoanalysis, the nineteenth and early twentieth centuries nurtured a wide-ranging culture of suspicion, fostering distrust of both society and individual. Sherlock Holmes is a paragon of this culture, particularly in his belief that things are never what they seem. "You look at these scattered country houses, and are impressed by their beauty," he tells Watson. "I look at them, and the only thought which comes to me is a feeling of their isolation and of the impunity with which crime may be committed there."[53]

In contrast, the forensic aesthetic seems to parallel a transition to a suburban, or postmodern, paranoia. The object of suspicion now seems to escape narrow boundaries and spill across the spectrum of contemporary life, so that Holmes's self-contained solutions appear impossibly quaint. Meanwhile Benjamin's suspiciousness has been institutionalized, built into a security-camera culture where innocent sites are considered potential crime scenes. A routine trip to the convenience store, for instance, involves walking through doors emblazoned with height strips designed to gauge the size of fleeing robbers.

Our suburban or decentered mode of paranoia is touched on in Ruscha's **Ruscha** cat. no. 66 *Three Murders* (1981), an absurdly attenuated horizontal picture of dismal, smog-shrouded suburban sprawl. No bloody events are depicted; on close inspection, however, one finds the word *murder* written in tiny black letters in three different places near the picture's bottom edge. Traceless acts of violence form an almost incidental part of the scenery of contemporary life, but Ruscha's bland-looking terrain—bereft of inhabitants, public spaces, or even clearly identifiable topography—does not conjure a real place. Its horizontal format parodies the scale of billboards and Cinemascope, and in the end it seems less like an actual landscape than a fatal emblem of the media-trained suburbanite's indifferently scanning gaze.

In *Three Murders* the word functions like a kind of blocking device, a graphic trap that—like our television screens—psychologically binds and blinds us with its seductive assurance that it leaves nothing out, that it communicates everything we need to know (an idea parodied by the picture's absurd horizontal thrust). Ruscha, here as in so much of his work, conjures the effects of living in our wall-to-wall media culture, where our environment—even its violence—is something we "read," a disembodied constellation of signs.

It is against precisely this background that the emergence of a forensic aesthetic makes sense. Faced with a mode of cultural experience that seems terminally, and seamlessly, alienated, it responds not with the modernist's cry of anguish, but by confronting us with the actions of a missing body or with incomplete scenes that must be reconstituted from shreds of evidence. It insists, in this indirect manner, that our corporeal existence is the inaccessible ground on which meaning is staged.

In considering the development of forensic strategies in postwar art, we began by surveying a transition from the tradition of the discrete object—the framed painting or pedestal-mounted sculpture—to an art of scattered and ambiguous clues, in which information seems to be straightforwardly presented but we are nevertheless denied the whole story. "What are the contents of any given sector of one's visual field?" Morris asked in regard to postminimalist art. "A heterogenous collection of substances and shapes, neither incomplete nor especially complete."[54]

This transition is not merely the tale of a genre's fall from grace, the decline in status of painting and traditional sculpture which has often been mistaken for their death. To understand its implications, we must see these formats from a broader perspective, as cultural models of framed order, autonomy, and categorical hygiene. Forensic modes of art, in contrast, lead us to consider the residue of a surrounding historical field.

In this respect this aesthetic forms part of a significant shift in the history of the relationship between viewer and artwork and reveals meridians of influence not usually acknowledged. A forensic tendency appears in radically different styles of art, yet if content is something that cannot be seen, then we should not be surprised if connections between such works are not always visible on the surface. As already discussed, what ultimately defines this aesthetic

66. Vija Celmins, *Tulip Car #1*, 1966 (cat. no. 20).

67. Nam June Paik performing La Monte Young's *Composition 1960 #10* for Robert Morris at Fluxus International Festpiel neuester Musik, Wiesbaden, 1962; photograph of performance.

68. Paul McCarthy; *Painting a White Line on the Floor with My Face*, 1973; photograph of a performance; courtesy Rosamund Felsen Gallery.

is not an approach to forms and materials, but the way viewers are positioned by the work—the art's public access, as it were. From Pollock's sublime abstractions to Harris's gritty cultural investigations, the viewer encounters scenes of aftermath in which he or she is immersed, whether in a field of swirling lines or a matrix of social reference.

Of equal weight is the forensic's emphasis on *physical* traces and the way it calls attention to the body's ghostly presence in an image-driven society. In contrast to much of the corporeal art from the last decade, which often tries to directly represent and "restore" the body, this vein of art functions like the chalk outline placed around the corpse at a crime scene. The body is envisioned neither as an innocent repository of nature nor as an existential symbol of isolation, but as an artifact that leaves traces and in turn is a surface for recording them. In the sublime chaos of Pollock's splattered paint, the forensic aesthetic finds a buried body that has been dissolved and dispersed. At the same time the forensic approach reminds us that our corporeal experience, our feelings of pain and pleasure, remains forever outside the domain of symbols. Indeed, this absence is the structural point, the black hole, around which our symbolic systems orbit.

Does the forensic mode, then, comprise a postmortem investigation of modernism itself? Certainly the viewer's role as investigator seems an apt one for probing the leftovers of modernist experience, the contradictory fragments and patchwork fabric of a "reality" in which pieces of the puzzle are consistently missing or seem to radically change meaning when viewed from another angle. In any event, by stressing the object's cluelike and contingent status, this strain of art encourages us to rehearse and reassess the ways in which we interpret our daily encounters with the world. And I hope that, as a metaphor, the notion of the forensic provides a useful framework for approaching contemporary art in an age when the visible has been discredited, when seeing is no longer believing. At such a moment, as the artists in this exhibition are well aware, we cannot help but have a vested interest in evidence of all kinds.

Notes

1. "Walter Benjamin's 'Short History of Photography,'" trans. Phil Patton, *Artforum* 15 (February 1977): 51.
2. Max Kozloff, "Nine in a Warehouse: An Attack on the Status of the Object," *Artforum* 7 (February 1969): 38.
3. As Klaus Kertess asked of Le Va's *Distributions*: "At what point does the material risk turning from being 'sculpture,' into becoming the vestige or trace of 'performance'?"; see Klaus Kertess, "Barry Le Va's Sculpture: Ellipsis and Ellipse," *Artforum* 21 (January 1983): 60.
4. Robert Pincus-Witten, introduction to *The New Sculpture, 1965–75: Between Geometry and Gesture*, exh. cat. (New York: Whitney Museum of American Art, 1990), 23.
5. Quoted in Robert Pincus-Witten, *Postminimalism into Maximalism: American Art, 1966–1986* (Ann Arbor: University of Michigan Research Press, 1987), 135.
6. See Kozloff, "Nine in a Warehouse," and Robert Morris, "Notes on Sculpture, Part 4: Beyond Objects," *Artforum* 7 (February 1969): 41.
7. Robert Morris, "Antiform," *Artforum* 6 (April 1968); reprinted in *The New Sculpture*, p. 100.
8. Harold Rosenberg, "The American Action Painters" (1952), in *The Tradition of the New* (New York: Horizon Press, 1959), 25.
9. David Humphrey, *Stained Sheets/Holy Shroud*, exh. cat. (Santa Monica, Calif.: Krygier/ Landau Contemporary Art, 1990), 3.
10. Alexandra Munroe, *Japanese Art after 1945: Scream against the Sky* (New York: Harry N. Abrams, 1994), 84. Other examples of a forensic aesthetic in Gutai art include the work of Kazuo Shiraga (see fig. 44), whose entire oeuvre "was painted with the artist's bare feet on unstretched canvas attached to the floor. Balancing on a hanging rope which he grasped with his fists, Shiraga dipped and swung his weight through the thick, wet oil paint. The finished painting stands as a record of his random spins, swirls, and slips" (ibid., 92). Ushio Shinohara, a member of Tokyo's Neo-Dada group, provocatively responded to Shiraga's work with his 1958 "boxing painting" performance: "half-naked with a mohawk hair-cut, Shinohara dipped his gloved fists into a bucket of paint and punched his way along an extensive sheet of canvas" (ibid., 97). Shiraga's work, it's worth noting, stands as a clear precedent to Carolee Schneemann's *Up to and Including Her Limits* (1973–76; fig. 39).
11. Leo Steinberg, *Other Criteria: Confrontations with Twentieth-Century Art* (New York: Oxford University Press, 1972), 216. It is worth noting that at the time homosexual acts were illegal in New York State; Rauschenberg's own bed was thus a regular crime scene.
12. Barbara Haskell and John G. Hanhardt, *Yoko Ono: Arias and Objects* (Salt Lake City: Gibbs Smith, 1991), 87. Ono's *Blood Piece* (1960) featured the text: "Use your blood to paint. Keep painting until you faint. (a). Keep painting until you die. (b)." For her *Smoke Painting* (1961; fig. 64) the

69. Terry Fox; *Asbestos Tracking*, 1970; performance, asbestos on concrete; courtesy Reese Palley Gallery, San Francisco.

viewer was asked to burn the canvas with a cigarette and watch the smoke; the work was finished when the "painting" turned to ashes.

13. Al Hansen, "London: Destruction in Art Symposium" (review), *Art News* 65 (November 1966): 58.

14. Brian O'Doherty, *Inside the White Cube: The Ideology of the Gallery Space* (San Francisco: Lapis Press, 1986), 75; Jane Livingstone, "Barry Le Va: Distributional Sculpture," *Artforum* 7 (November 1968): 66.

15. Quoted in Robert Storr, "An Interview with Ilya Kabakov," *Art in America* 83 (January 1995): 64.

16. Conversation with the author, London, 21 December 1996.

17. See Malcolm Gladwell, "Crime as Epidemic," *New Yorker*, 3 June 1996, 38: "In a famous experiment conducted twenty-seven years ago by the Stanford University psychologist Philip Zimbardo, a car was parked on a street in Palo Alto, where it sat untouched for a week. At the same time, Zimbardo had an identical car parked in a roughly comparable neighborhood in the Bronx, only in this case the license plates were removed and the hood propped open. Within a day, it was stripped. Then, in a final twist, Zimbardo smashed one of the Palo Alto car's windows with a sledgehammer. Within a few hours, that car, too, was destroyed."

18. Black, *Aesthetics of Murder*, 52.

19. O'Doherty, *Inside the White Cube*, 75

20. Ibid., 75, 64.

21. Le Va, in Pincus-Witten, *Postminimalism into Maximalism,* 135.

22. Robert Morris, "Notes on Sculpture, Part 4: Beyond Objects" (1968), in *The New Sculpture,* 181.

23. Allan Kaprow, *Assem-blages, Installations, and Environments* (New York: Harry N. Abrams, 1966), 165, 154.

24. Ibid., 165.

25. O'Doherty, *Inside the White Cube,* 65.

26. My thanks to Karen Jacobson for pointing out the Latin roots of *forensic.*

27. Henry McBride, *New York Sun,* 23 December 1950; cited in Rosalind Krauss, *The Optical Unconscious* (Cambridge: MIT Press, 1993), 323.

28. Walter Benjamin, "Paris, Capital of the Nineteenth Century," in *Reflections: Essays, Aphorisms, Autobiographical Writings,* ed. Peter Demetz, trans. Edmund Jephcott (New York: Schocken Books, 1986), 155.

29. Marioni titled this artwork *The Act of Drinking Beer with Friends Is the Highest Form of Art* (1970). In the same year Terry Fox executed *Asbestos Tracking* (fig. 69) at the Reese Palley Gallery: after dipping his shoes in asbestos, he skipped and shuffled across the gallery floor, leaving toxic footprints as a record of the event.

30. The fingerprint as motif can be traced back to Pollock, interestingly enough. Following Hans Hoffman's *Third Hand* (1947), which included an impression of the artist's paint-smeared digits, Pollock left his palm prints on *Number 1, 1948,* and a handprint three years later on *One (No. 31).* As a figure of speech, "the touch of the hand" referred to the individuality of an artist's brush strokes, yet here it seemingly indicated that evidence was needed to confirm the artist's physical existence and, in a last-gasp effort, assert his unique identity. Pollock framed this threat in existential terms, which is to say that his work omits any allusion to the social forces that might make the body seem an endangered artifact. By the mid-1940s, however, our society's reign of mass-media spectacle was already firmly in place, along with the subsequent fallout, a nuclear cloud of uncertainty that colors corporeal and empirical experience.

31. Baldessari's *White Shape* (1984; fig. 27, cat. no. 6) potently alludes to this fatal connection: it consists of a photo of Pollock posing in his studio between a "drip" painting on the floor and one on the wall behind him, but Baldessari has blotted out the artist's body with white paint. On one level this intervention obliterates what was a heroic image of Pollock; yet given the formal kinship of the artist's paintings with blood-spattered floors and walls, the altered photograph hints that the linking of art and action subtly transforms the studio into a forensic site.

32. Philip Kerr, *A Philosophical Investigation* (New York: Farrar, Straus, Giroux, 1993), 166.

33. Charles Desmarais, *Proof: Los Angeles Art and Photography, 1960–1980,* exh. cat. (Los Angeles: Fellows of Contemporary Art, 1992), 86.

34. Kerr, *Philosophical Investigation,* 166.

35. Slajov Zizek, *Looking Awry: An Introduction to Jacques Lacan through Popular Culture* (Cambridge: MIT Press, 1992), 143.

36. See Michael Fried, "Art and Objecthood" (1967), in *Minimal Art,* ed. Gregory Battock (New York: Dutton, 1968), 116–47.

37. Robert L. Pincus, *On a Scale That Competes with the World: The Art of Edward and Nancy Reddin Kienholz* (Berkeley and Los Angeles: University of California Press, 1990), 82. Although, as Pincus has pointed out, it may be closer to a form of stop-action theater, a frozen tableau made up of grotesque, surreal figures and "archaeological" artifacts from the modern world (26).

38. Ilya Kabakov, *On the "Total" Installation* (Bonn: Cantz, 1995), 248.

39. O'Doherty, *Inside the White Cube*, 9.

40. Rosenberg, "American Action Painters," 35. Rosenberg bewailed the appearance of "modern architecture, not only for sophisticated homes, but for corporations, municipalities, synagogues; Modern furniture and crockery in mail-order catalogues; Modern vacuum cleaners, can openers; beer-ad 'mobiles'—along with reproductions and articles on advanced painting in big-circulation magazines."

41. In Calvin Tompkins, *The Bride and Her Bachelors: Five Masters of the Avant-Garde* (New York: Penguin, 1976), 67.

42. Benjamin Buchloh, "The Italian Metamorphosis, 1943–1968" (review), *Artforum* 33 (January 1995): 83. Not even their collectors, after all, could directly encounter the bodily wastes that Manzoni repackaged—not, that is, without destroying the work itself. All one could truly possess was the inaccessible residue of an absent body.

43. William O'Green, introduction to *Ars Criminalis*, by John Strange, cited in Ellery Queen, *The French Powder Mystery* (New York: New American Library, 1969), 82.

44. William Wilson, "Lewis Baltz Photos: The Landscape as Scapegoat," *Los Angeles Times*, 31 March 1992, F16.

45. See Roland Barthes, *Camera Lucida* (New York: Hill and Wang, 1981).

46. Zizek, *Looking Awry*, 58.

47. Cited in Peter Brooks, "Paranoids All," *Times Literary Supplement*, 27 September 1996, 30.

48. Of course, other issues were at stake in *La Filature*. It is hard to imagine a male artist executing a similar project: as a woman followed by an unknown male voyeur, Calle played on the way women are often viewed by men in a predatory manner. And in a world of anonymous citizens, whose existence is not suspect when undocumented? Yet it is also significant that Calle was unaware of her pursuer's identity: shadowed by a stranger, she was thus confronted with the possibility that any of the unknown persons around her could be the "chosen one" whose unseen gaze would verify her existence. Indeed, the project's goal, the artist later said, was to provide photographic evidence of her existence. In this case the concerns of forensic-style art had apparently evolved from recording traces of artistic process to offering proof of the artist's very identity.

49. Black, *Aesthetics of Murder*, 3. As Black points out, we can deny the crime scene's aesthetic impact only by counterfeiting a "pure" morality that disavows the full range of our emotional response. This entails a kind of murder, a killing off of awareness and the freedom it potentially brings to the ongoing investigation that constitutes our existence. Morality is a public matter, yet as the forensic approach insists, aesthetics is a bodily discourse and so can never be completely subsumed within the former sphere. Instead it suggests that morality and aesthetics are

70. Gary Simmons; sketch for *Step in the Arena (The Essentialist Trap)*, 1994; charcoal on vellum; 20 x 24 in. (50.8 x 61 cm); courtesy the artist and Metro Pictures.

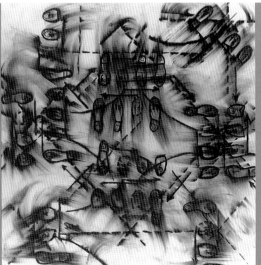

not always reconcilable aspects of human experience, but make up semiautonomous realms, interlocking and overlapping at certain points, diverging at others.

This notion runs counter to the main legacy of modernism, so many varieties of which attempted to fuse aesthetic and moral perspectives. From the Bauhaus concept of architecture as social engineering to Clement Greenberg's notion of art as a self-referential research into its own materials, modernism betrays a concern with spiritual hygiene ("integrity" is a frequent code word for this obsession with clean borders) that is as closely related to moral issues as to anything purely aesthetic. The "purity" of art for art's sake is nothing if not a moral posture. Meanwhile, that other great modernist dream—the fusion of art and life championed by everyone from dadaists and constructivists to surrealists and on up to the architects of Happenings and performance rituals—proposes a model of existence where distinctions between morality and aesthetics would automatically dissolve. It is worth noting that this same dream was also pursued under those exemplary modernist systems, communism and fascism, both of which tried to obliterate, in different ways, divisions between aesthetic and moral spheres (as Walter Benjamin famously quipped, fascism aestheticizes politics, while communism politicizes art).

50. Thomas De Quincey, *The Confessions of an English Opium-Eater and Other Essays* (London: Macmillan and Co., 1901), 283.

51. Jack Katz, *Seductions of Crime: Moral and Sensual Attractions in Doing Evil* (New York: Basic Books, 1988).

52. Jean Baudrillard, *The Perfect Crime*, trans. Chris Turner (London: Verso, 1996), 3.

53. Arthur Conan Doyle, *Sherlock Holmes: The Complete Novels and Stories*, vol. 1 (New York: Bantam Classics, 1986), 438.

54. Morris, "Notes on sculpture," 183.

71. John Baldessari; *Art Disaster: Evidence*, 1971 (cat. no. 3).

Plates

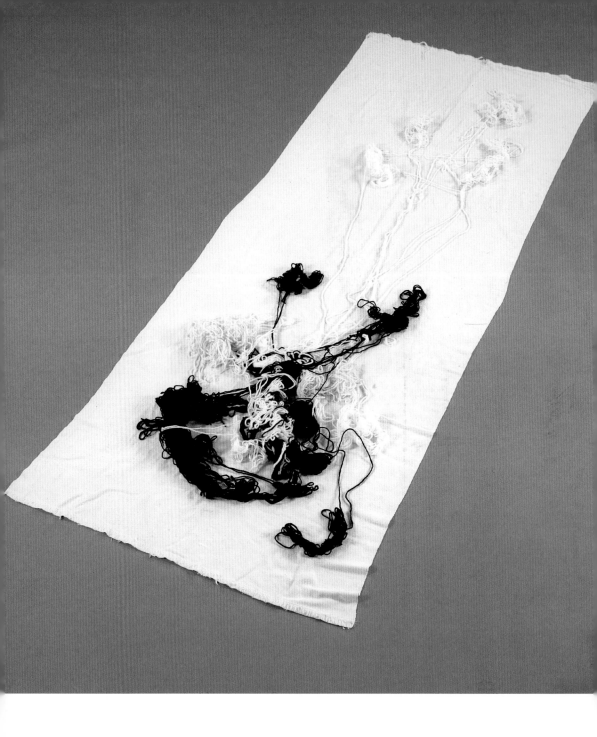

72. Mike Kelley
Yarn #3, 1990
(cat. no. 42)

73. Mike Mandel and Larry Sultan
Untitled, from *Evidence*, 1977
(cat. no. 51)

74. Edward Kienholz and Nancy Reddin Kienholz
White Easel with Machine Pistol, 1975
(cat. no. 44)

76. James Luna
The Tribal Identity, 1995
(cat. no. 48)

77. Richard Misrach
Playboy #42 (Rambo), 1989–91
(cat. no. 55)

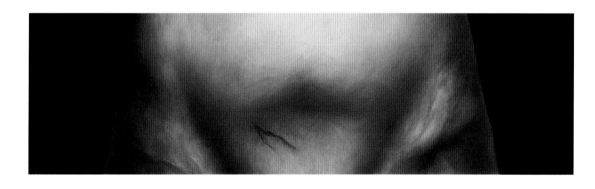

78. Monica Majoli
Untitled, 1990
(cat. no. 49)

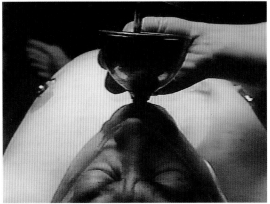

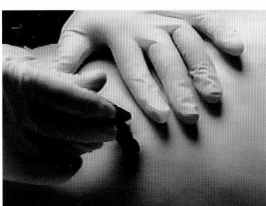
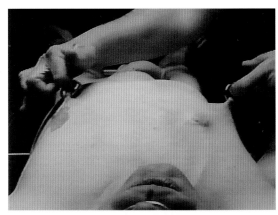

79. Bob Flanagan and Sheree Rose
Autopsy, 1994 (stills from video)
(cat. no. 30)

80. Michelle Rollman
Untitled (Instrument Case), 1995
(cat. no. 63)

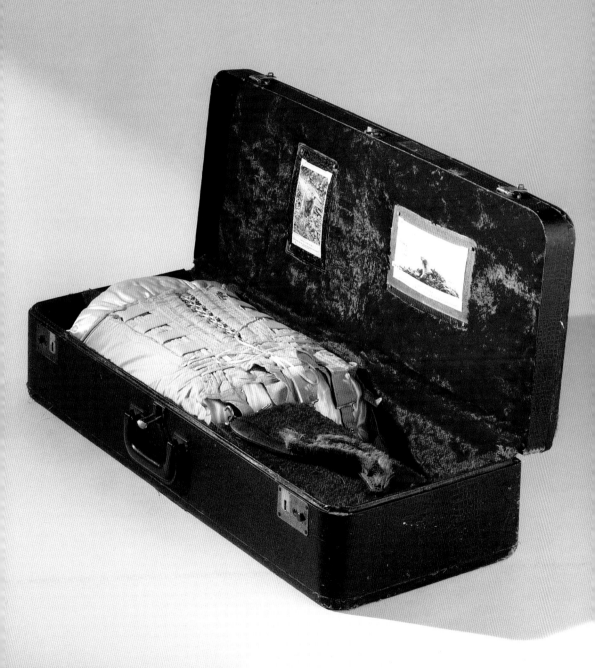

81. Richard Hawkins
Poison, 1991
(cat. no. 36)

82. George Stone
Unknown, Unwanted, Unconscious, Untitled,
1993
(cat. no. 68)

83. Sharon Lockhart
Untitled, 1996
(cat. no. 47)

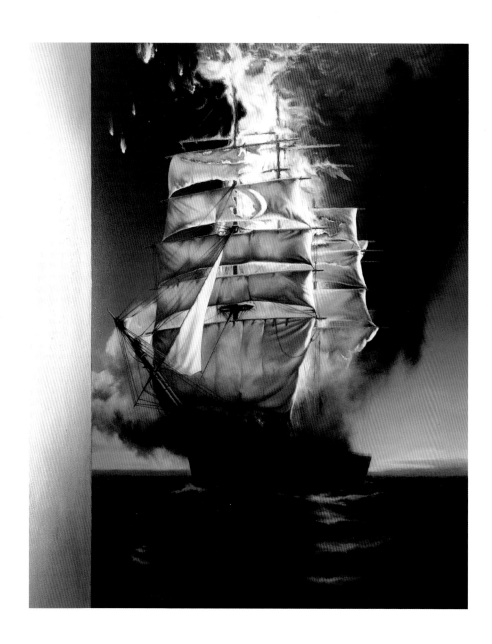

84. Nancy Reese
El Señor, 1990
(cat. no. 62)

85. Eileen Cowin
Untitled, 1997
(cat. no. 22)

86. Vincent Fecteau
Shirley Temple Room #8, 1994
(cat. no. 29)

87. D-L Alvarez
The Boomin System (Hold On I'm Coming), 1995
(installation view)
(cat. no. 2)

88. Paul McCarthy
Santa Chocolate Shop, 1996–97 (still from video)
(cat. no. 52)

89. Lyle Ashton Harris
The Watering Hole VIII, 1996
(cat. no. 35)

The Exhaustion of Space at the Scene of the Crime

Anthony Vidler

The question of the exact position of the X that in common lore supposedly marks the most significant spot at the scene of a crime has more often than not been in doubt. Precise in terminology—and, of course, in geometrical accuracy—the spot has been, so to speak, on the move throughout the last century and a half of modern criminological practice. The location of the body might be marked by tape and chalk on the ground to which it has fallen; the alleged site of the crime might be gridded with painstaking care in order to provide a coordinate system by which to situate the evidence, carefully collected in labeled bags for presentation in court; the tracks of the criminal, the traces of blood, the dispersed weapons, and expended ammunition might all be gathered together and plotted on the special kind of map that criminologists have deemed appropriate to define the "scene" of the crime in legally tenable terms. But all this precision, as fictional and real prosecutors since Edgar Allan Poe's Dupin and Arthur Conan Doyle's Holmes have found, falls apart at the moment space enters into the equation. That is to say, while the question of "what" has usually been answered easily enough through physical evidence (at least until the most sophisticated technologies, such as those of DNA analysis, have proved too much beyond a doubt to be believable), the question of "where" has often been rendered unanswerable by the simple trick of denouncing the various projections, suppositions, and assumptions that underlie any exercise in mapping. Objects can be presented in the courtroom, but spaces always have to be imagined—and represented. And representation has, from at least the early nineteenth century, been not so much a science as an art controlled by psychological projection and careful artifice.

This was no doubt the message of the writer Georges Bataille, when—in his brief review of the photographic album *X Marks the Spot*,[1] published in *Documents* in 1930—he remarked on the custom of publishing photographs of criminal cadavers, a practice "that seemed equally popular in Europe, certainly representing a considerable moral transformation in the attitude of the public to violent death."[2] To illustrate the point, Bataille selected an image from this "first photographic history of Chicago gangland slayings," depicting the corpse of an assassinated gangster found in the ice of Lake Michigan, the figure face up, as if frozen while floating, a literal monument to its own death.

In one sense, of course, this image has no relation to the concept of "x marks the spot," announced in the title of the album, which refers to the custom of marking the position of the victim after the removal of the body; there was in this case no mark to be left on the ice following the excavation of the frozen corpse, and its place of discovery was destined to be effaced forever with the subsequent thaw. For an instant, then, the corpse acted as its own mark, one to be rendered permanent only in the police photo. And this photograph, as Georges Didi-Huberman recently pointed out, was itself an enigmatic record: "First, one doesn't see very much, insofar as the image evokes a pure and simple site, albeit a chaotic one, a black-and-white magma. Then one recognizes the drowned (and presumably assassinated) man *trapped in the ice* of Lake Michigan."[3] Transformed into an anamorphic vision by virtue of the flattening surface of the ice and the angle of the photo, the dead gangster has been doubly recomposed— first, as a marker of the site of his own death and, second, as a visually encoded "hieroglyphic" image of that mark. Further, whatever place was marked by the position of the body, it was not the site of the assassination itself, but rather the place where the gangster had ended up, propelled by the currents of the lake and frozen by chance on rising to the surface—a mark therefore of the ever-exilic, ever-transitory place of death in modern urban life and, at the same time, of the consistent popular and judicial fascination with the nature and signs of that place.

Put in terms of a criminal investigation—the forensic study of the "scene of the crime" preparatory to bringing a suspect to trial—Bataille's scenario would certainly be troubling to a police method that relied on physical evidence

90. Jasper Johns; *Painting Bitten by a Man*, 1961; encaustic on canvas; 9½ x 6⅞ in. (24.1 x 17.5 cm); collection of the artist. ©1997 Jasper Johns/Licensed by VAGA, New York, NY.

faithfully collected and recorded by that instrument of the "real," the camera. The distortion of the visual field produced an image that could be reassembled into the figure of a corpse only through an equal and opposite distortion, a sideways reading, so to speak, that in itself cast doubt on the original form. Furthermore, at the same time that the site of the discovery of the body acted as the stable context for inferring the nature and perpetrator of the murder, its unstable coordinates unfixed the evidence and disseminated the clues into a spatial void. *Space*, infiltrating and dispersing *place,* put the tangibility and thereby the veracity of courtroom "exhibits" into doubt. The crime takes place in space, which in turn renders its exact position unstable.

And yet this very spatial dimension of crime, a commonplace of city novels from Poe's "Paris" and Conan Doyle's "London" to Chandler's "Los Angeles," has been largely overlooked in criticism in favor of the material evidence presented by traces and objects, a preoccupation shared by the police and recently underlined in the heated debates over the "bloody glove" in the O. J. Simpson trial. In that trial the "fit" of the glove and its possible purchase by Simpson were less important in the end than its position in space, its potential for having been "planted." Its obvious immobility in the evidence photos was disturbed by the defense's clever manipulation of its equally obvious potential for movement. Similarly, blood, which indelibly marked socks and vans belonging to the accused, thus creating a trail that police hoped would trace the crime back to the culprit, was demonstrated to be equally mobile, as it moved from site to station to laboratory and back to crime site again. Indeed, the entire trial was destabilized by a defense that exploited space against object, that knew how to set in motion every fixed premise and stable clue by situating it in a field of other spaces and sites which raised the possibility of doubt as to its fixed place. The fluidity of space was pitched against the stability of place, the object consistently displaced by its spatial field.

Here we are reminded of that canonical tale of spatial displacement, Poe's "The Purloined Letter," later to be reconstituted as a psychoanalytical fable of automatism of repetition by Jacques Lacan in 1956.[4] Poe's very title, Lacan cautions, is a clue to the story's implications: he points out that the word *purloined,* translated by Charles Baudelaire as *volée* (stolen), is derived from the Anglo-French *pur* (as in *purpose, purchase, purport*) and the Old French *loing, loigner, longé* ("alongside"), making a word that implies the action of "putting aside," "putting alongside," or even "put in the wrong place." Such attributes of displacement, when joined to the action of "stealing"—for purloining also implies a theft, if not one involving outright confiscation—intimates the complex matrix of intersecting double scenes staged by Poe's narrative. The first (Lacan significantly terms it the "primal scene"), in the royal boudoir (perfect scene for a primal crime), finds the Queen receiving a letter, surprised by the King, and in confusion "hiding" the letter by leaving it open on a table, only to witness the Minister substitute his own letter for hers and make off with it, together with the power that its ownership conveys. The second (a repetition of the first) is set in the Minister's apartment and stages Dupin discovering the letter in full view, hanging from the mantel, and himself substituting a letter with a motto for the Minister to reflect upon when opening what he thinks is the Queen's. These two spaces of "putting in the wrong (therefore the right) place," of staging the evidence in full view so as to hide it from those who would think it hidden, are separated in Poe's story by the intermission—a scene of search, of a relentlessly thorough police investigation, one that, as the Prefect of Police has to admit, comes up empty-handed.

The premise of this search is simple enough and has been repeated to infinity. Anticipating that a clever thief would hide his spoils cleverly, the police "search *everywhere*." "Everywhere" for Poe, and for the Prefect, involves a scientific survey of every possible space: the entire building is searched, room by room, the furniture first. Every possible drawer is opened on the premise that "such a thing as a *'secret'* drawer is impossible" to conceal against a method that measures accurately "the fiftieth part of a line" in order to account for the mathematically calculated bulk of every compartment. Even the space behind and between books, the space in the binding and the pages, is submitted to this probing inspection. The surface of the house itself is "divided . . . into compartments," which are numbered, and "each individual square inch throughout the premises, including the two houses immediately adjoining," is scrutinized with a microscope (212). This search would be, Lacan remarks, a veritable "exhaustion of space," whereby the entire "field in which the police presume, not without reason, that the letter should be found" is submitted to a kind of quadrillage of exactitude in such a way that "had the letter been deposited within the range of their search" the police would have found it.[5]

We should not be surprised to find the Prefect's search methods systematically taught in contemporary police practice: the training manual *Basic Course Unit Guide: Crime Scene Search Technique,* developed for the California Commission on Peace Officer Standards and Training, advocates geometrically controlled search patterns (as opposed to a "point-to-point" search, which is

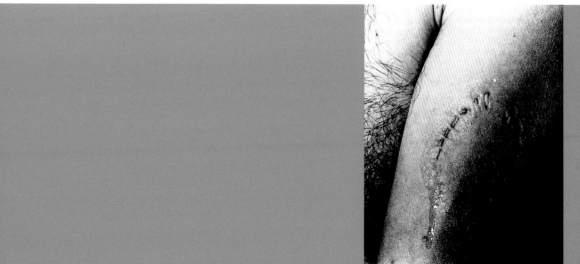

91. Vito Acconci; *Trademarks* (detail), 1970; photographed activity, ink prints; courtesy Barbara Gladstone Gallery, New York.

"very often disorganized"), such as the "strip search" in lanes defined by stakes and lines; the "double strip (grid)" search; the "quadrant (or sector)" search, which in indoor situations would divide the "building into rooms," the "book-shelf into sections," and the "cupboard into [gridded] sections"; the "circular (spiral or concentric)" search; the "wheel (or radiate)" search; the "area search"; and, finally, the aerial search. Tips for teaching these methods describe how students should test each search method in the context of specific rooms and spaces, carefully photographing, sketching, describing in notes, collecting, marking, and preserving the resulting "evidence."[6]

Poe's spatial field of crime scenes is, in a similar sense, three-dimensional; both the map constructed by the police search, and the map of the displaced, purloined letter, are construed in space and time (the one—we will find the letter given time; the other—the letter will never be found because not "looked for" in the right field), so that the eventual intersection of the two fields effectuated by Dupin results in a kind of warping, producing a Klein bot-tle form that returns the letter to its receiver, but by a path that twists the space of purloining to enter and exit Dupin's own desk. The poetics of crime and its revelation transform the geometrical space of rational detection into a knot of abyssal proportions.

It is worth noting, in the context of this exhibition, that Dupin's success was not a triumph of visual acuity; he did not see the letter with any more precision than the Prefect. Rather, his feat was the result of intellectual intro-jection, precisely a feat of not seeing, conducted in a black box specifically set up for reflection, not vision: Dupin's "little back library, or book closet," surrounded by "curling eddies of smoke," with the two friends "sitting in the dark." "If there is any point requiring reflection," observed Dupin, as he forbore to enkindle the wick, "we shall examine it to better purpose in the dark" (208).

Such a refusal of vision, in favor of interior reflection, is consistent with the arguments of Walter Benjamin, himself an avid student of Dupin, that space, or rather "architecture," is experienced primarily in a state of "distraction," a state that ignores the visual characteristics of the building in favor of its haptic and tactile environment, a "dark space" as Eugène Minkowski would have it, where vision is unconscious and "losing one's way" is the key to knowledge. In the same vein, Dupin notes the peculiar characteristic of "overly-large lettered signs and placards of the street," which, like the purloined letter, "escape observation by dint of being excessively obvious" (219). Indeed, we might infer that the thorough spatial search launched by the Prefect was itself less visual than methodical, a search conducted according to habitual and customary premises. After all, the crime itself was accomplished in full view of the victim and seen by her, and the perpetrator was content to leave the stolen letter equally in full view.

Lacan's identification of the three kinds of gaze characterizing the intersub-jectivity of the scenes of Poe's narrative supports this interpretation of the "unseeing" look. According to Lacan, "the first is a gaze that sees nothing: that of the King and of the police"; "the second, a gaze that sees that the first sees

92. Chris Burden; *Shoot*, 1971; black-and-white photograph of performance at F Space, November 19, 1971; courtesy the artist.

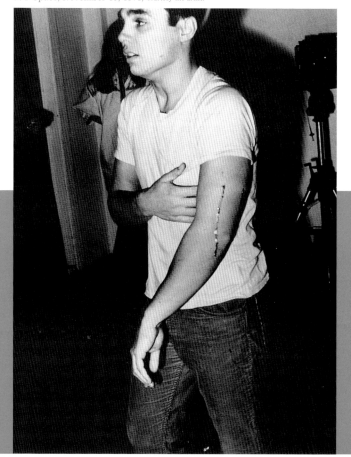

nothing and deceives itself in seeing hidden what it hides—the queen and the minister"; "the third sees that the first two gazes leave what is to be hidden exposed to whomever would seize it—the minister and Dupin."

When set in a spatial field, whether enclosed or open, this unconscious blindness becomes a pathological condition that late nineteenth-century analysts would identify as a return to the haptic, a tactophilia that, in its "close-up" vision, approximated the early stage of child development or, as applied to the history of vision by Alois Riegl, the optical structure of ancient Egypt. Only a haptic-driven optics, Riegl argued, could produce works like the pyramids, which revealed themselves in their three-dimensional totality to a viewer standing at their base—almost touching; a Greek temple, by contrast, demanded to be viewed from a "normal" distance and in three-quarter view. Late Roman monuments required neither a close-up nor a normal vantage point, but rather confused the viewer by (as in the case of the cylindrical Pantheon) oscillating between figure and ground or, more precisely, by providing no fixed ground against which to be seen.[7]

Riegl's analysis, while obviously oversimplified in its reliance on a biological model of development, nevertheless contains the premise, utilized by cultural critics and artists throughout the twentieth century, that vision—which has a "history," as Victor Burgin has stressed[8]—is always confused by its unconscious, its determining relations to touch and the other nonvisual senses, when, as a bodily projection, it finds itself in space. Thus, against the optical stupidity of the police—interested, as Fredric Jameson points out in his brilliant essay on Chandler,[9] more in the control of administration than in the prevention of crime—is posed the intuitive brilliance of the detective, the optical unconscious's underdog: Dupin, Holmes, Marlowe et al.

Los Angeles, of course, has been the site of criminal spatial dissemination par excellence. As Jameson has noted, it is Los Angeles, more than any other city, that has consistently, since the 1930s, anticipated the breakdown of class and character-type division embedded in the more stratified cities of old Europe, a breakdown that is precisely the result of its spatial character—"a spreading out horizontally, a flowing apart of the elements of the social structure." The unstructured nature of the city and its society drives the detective into space, so to speak: no longer, as with Dupin and Holmes, confined to the space of his own mental analysis and problem solving—the intuitive rationalist, the mathematician of chance—the Los Angeles detective "is propelled outwards into the space of his world and obliged to move from one kind of social reality to another incessantly, trying to find clues." Time and space become commingled in a complex narrative where the murder, to take an example at random, is committed only at the end of the book, rendering it a "senseless accident" rather than, as classically the case, the ultimate object of the search. Similarly, the objects that once formed a growing body of evidence—of clues painstakingly collected, tabulated, and preserved—now are described and "collected" for the sake not of the search but of a generalized sense of place, a nostalgia for products, often entirely incidental to the case at hand, representing the author's knowledge of the world he evokes and authenticating a picaresque narrative for its own sake: "The author's task is to make an inventory of these objects, to demonstrate by the fullness of his catalogue, how completely he knows his way around the world of machines and machine products, and it is in this sense that Chandler's descriptions of furniture, his description of women's clothing styles, will function: as a naming, a sign of expertise and know-how."[10]

These objects, then, have lost the fetish character of clues and certainly no longer carry the fetish character of their status as products, but instead gain in their generalized dissemination through the space of the novel, an overwhelming aura of criminality pe se, as if every beer bottle, cigarette, ashtray, and car were invested with a potential seediness, as if even the spaces in which they are set, the rundown motels, the nondescript bars, the diners, were carriers of a low-grade criminal infection that has transformed the entire city into a scene of perpetual and undifferentiated crime. Even the space of the law was contaminated by such ubiquity of the lawless: a space that was to be identified, as Chandler himself noted, with the precinct station: "beyond the green lights of the precinct station you pass clear out of this world into a place beyond the law."[11] For Chandler and Los Angeles in general, this place has passed into the world itself.

As we have seen, Bataille's interest in gangland photos took its inspiration from this sense of the latent criminality of space. His observations on the gangster photo album were set in the context of his inquiry into architectural monumentality and the nature of public space in modern culture, an investigation begun in the articles "Architecture," "Espace" (Space), and "Musée" (Museum) in *Documents* and continued, as Denis Hollier has demonstrated, throughout his writings.[12] Here Bataille began to explore that profound destabilization of the realm of the monumental operated by the force of space itself and, more precisely, the psychological power of space considered as a fluid,

93. Nayland Blake; *El Dorado*, 1994 (cat. no. 14).

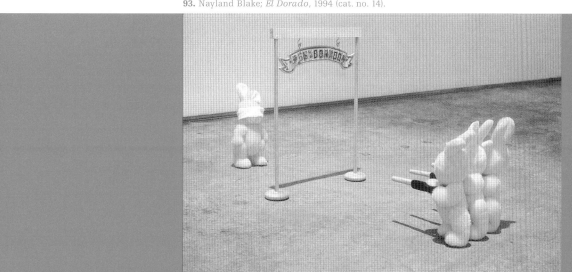

boundary-effacing, always displaced and displacing medium. In his brief article on space, published in the first issue of *Documents* in 1930, Bataille characterizes space as a "loutish" and errant child of philosophy, a breaker of protocol and an offender against propriety, a "scalawag at odds with society."[13] Its most powerful distinguishing quality was its "discontinuity."

A clue to Bataille's meaning may be gleaned from his first qualification of the word *espace* as "question des convenances," or a question of suitability. *Convenance* had long been, in architecture especially, a loaded term referring to the classical codes of appropriateness of a genre or an order to a particular program—at its simplest regulating the application of the orders and constraining decoration to a rigid social hierarchy. But evidently the *convenances* of which Bataille speaks are very different from those of the classical canon or, rather, even as they rely on former canons, are conceived in order to establish entirely new mixed genres and canons, not of social hierarchy, but of its dissolution; not of social propriety, but of its withering away—new genres and canons, that is, of power and eroticism represented in space, precisely through the ability of space itself to dissolve boundaries, as, that is, transgressive by nature, breaking the boundaries of all conventions, social or physical.

Rather than the dignified astronomical and geometrical entity imagined by the philosophers, space was in fact a bad object—abject and ignoble in its ubiquity, endlessly invading the protected realms of society and civilization with the disruptive forces of nature. As the images illustrating Bataille's article demonstrate, space was for him a vehicle of masquerade ("it seems that an ape dressed as a woman is no more than a division of space," runs the caption to a photograph of a chimpanzee dressed like a traditional maid, with shopping basket, seated in a jungle setting). It is equally a ritual of sexual initiation ("space... takes the form of an ignoble initiation rite") or, alternatively, of cannibalism ("space might become a fish swallowing another"). Finally, space would be the instrument that undermines the very foundations of lawful society. A fourth photograph, of the collapse of a prison in Columbus, Ohio, is given a caption drawn from the last paragraph of the article: "Obviously it will never enter anybody's head to lock the professors up in prison *to teach them what space is* (the day, for example, the walls collapse before the bars of their dungeons)."[14]

Space has thus not only confounded the geometers, it has demonstrated its disruptive power in the face of the most defended of institutions, reducing, so to speak, the Benthamite panopticon, constructed according to the laws of classical optics, to a formless heap of rubble. In this sense, Bataille argues, space is "pure violence," escaping time and geometry to affirm its presence as the expression of the *here-now*, the instantaneous, the simultaneous, and, by extension, the event. Space would not simply be an agent of the *informe*—a "formless" recently reconstrued by Yve-Alain Bois and Rosalind Krauss as a key to the rereading of what they see as a continuously present countercurrent in the avant-garde art of the twentieth century—but also the virulent and ubiquitous instrument of Bataille's campaign against objecthood, on behalf of the erosion of all conventional boundaries.[15]

Notes

1. *X Marks the Spot: Chicago Gang Wars in Pictures* (Chicago: Spot Publishing Co., 1930). The context for the enormous popularity of pulp presentations of gangsterdom and the "invention" of gangster mythology is well described in David E. Ruth, *Inventing the Public Enemy: The Gangster in American Culture, 1918–1934* (Chicago: University of Chicago Press, 1996), esp. 118–43.

2. Georges Bataille, *Œuvres complètes*, vol. 1, *Premiers écrits, 1922–1940* (Paris: Gallimard, 1973), 256; this article was first published in *Documents* 2, no. 7 (1930): 437–38.

3. Georges Didi-Huberman, *La Ressemblance informe ou le gai savoir visuel selon Georges Bataille* (Paris: Macula, 1995), 154.

4. Jacques Lacan, "Seminar on 'The Purloined Letter,'" trans. Jeffrey Mehlman, in *The Poetics of Murder,* ed. Glenn W. Most and William W. Stowe (New York: Harcourt Brace Jovanovich, 1983), 21–54; translation of "Le Séminaire sur 'La Lettre volée,'" in *Ecrits*, vol. 1 (Paris: Editions du Seuil, 1966). Quotations from "The Purloined Letter" are from *The Complete Tales and Poems of Edgar Allan Poe* (New York: Modern Library, 1938).

5. Lacan, "Seminar on 'The Purloined Letter,'" 33.

6. *Basic Course Unit Guide: Crime Scene Search Technique* (Commission on Peace Officer Standards and Training, c. 1985), 43.4–7.

7. See Alois Riegl, *Late Roman Art Industry,* trans. Rolf Winkes (Rome: Giorgio Bretschneider, 1985).

8. See Victor Burgin, "Geometry at an Amjection," in *Psychoanalysis and Cultural Theory: Thresholds,* ed. James Donald (London: Macmillan, 1991), 12.

9. Fredric Jameson, "On Raymond Chandler," in Most and Stowe, eds., *Poetics of Murder*.

10. Ibid., 127, 144, 138.

11. Cited without reference in ibid., 128.

12. See Denis Hollier, *La Prise de la Concorde: Essais sur Georges Bataille* (Paris: Gallimard, 1974), recently published in English translation under the title *Against Architecture: The Writings of Georges Bataille,* trans. Betsy Wing (Cambridge: MIT Press, 1989).

13. Georges Bataille, "Space," in *Encyclopedia Acephalica*, ed. Robert Lebel and Isabelle Waldberg (London: Atlas Press, 1995), 75.

14. Ibid., 77.

15. See Yve-Alain Bois and Rosalind Krauss, "A User's Guide to Entropy," *October,* no. 78 (Fall 1996): 55–56. Bois sees Bataille as working against architecture as an anthropomorphic image but retreating before the implications of this attack. Here I would simply point to the insidious powers of "space" in Bataille's construction and its consequent undermining of human institutions and bodies. Perhaps the point is somewhere in between: that, for Bataille, "space," properly *un*defined, was inevitably going to undo man's work with little need of help from the critic.

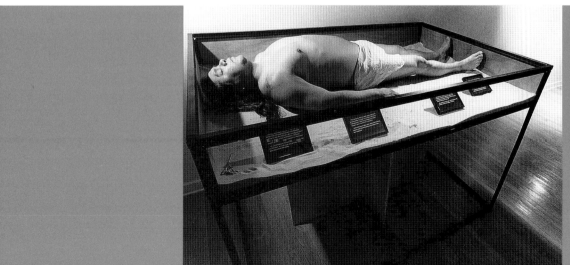

94. James Luna; *The Artifact Piece*, 1986; performance at the Museum of Man, San Diego; courtesy the artist.

95. Jacques-Louis David; *Marat assassiné (The Death of Marat)*, 1793; oil on canvas; 65 x 50½ in. (165.1 x 128.3 cm); Musées Royaux des Beaux-Arts de Belgique.

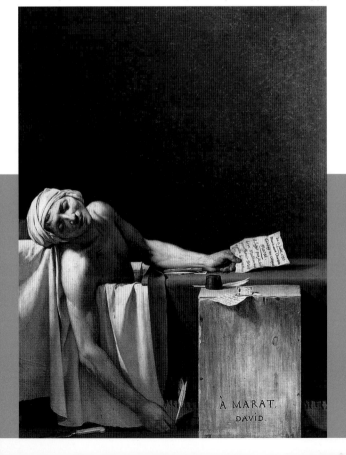

Checklist of the Exhibition

Terry Allen
(b. Witchita, Kansas, 1943)
1. Memory House, 1973
Photo and collage on paper
18 x 23 in. (45.7 x 58.4 cm)
Collection of the artist

D-L Alvarez
(b. Stockton, California, 1962)
2. The Boomin System (Hold On
I'm Coming), 1995
Mixed-media installation
Dimensions variable
Courtesy Nao Bustamonte and
Jack Hanley Gallery

John Baldessari
(b. National City, California, 1931)
3. Art Disaster: Evidence, 1971
Photograph on board
19¾ x 13⅜ in. (50.2 x 34 cm)

Collection of the artist; courtesy
Sonnabend Gallery, New York and
Margo Leavin Gallery, Los Angeles
4. Free Rolling Tire, 1971–72
Six black-and-white photographs
mounted on board, printed text
16 x 23¾ in. (40.6 x 60.3 cm) each
Sonnabend Gallery, New York
5. Violent Space Series: Nine Feet
(of Victim and Crowd) Arranged
by Position in Scene, 1976
Black-and-white photographs
mounted on board
24⅜ x 56½ in. (61.9 x 143.5 cm)
overall
Collection Robert H. Halff
6. White Shape, 1984
Black-and-white photograph with
acrylic, mounted on board
48 x 29 in. (121.9 x 73.7 cm)
Anonymous loan

96. Hiroshi Sugimoto; *The Brides in the Bath Murderer*, 1994; silver print;
20 x 24 in. (50.8 x 61 cm); courtesy Sonnabend Gallery, New York.

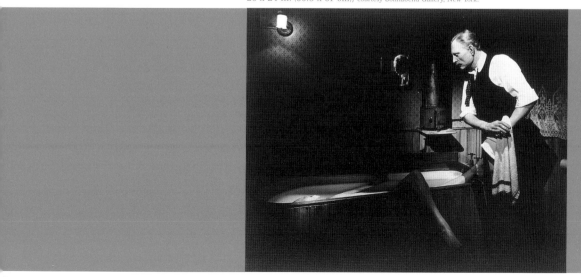

Lewis Baltz
(b. Newport Beach, California, 1945)
7. 11777 Foothill Boulevard, Los Angeles, CA, 1991 (printed 1992)
Silver dye-bleach (Cibachrome) print, ed. 1/3
50 x 98 in. (127 x 248.9 cm) framed
Los Angeles County Museum of Art, commissioned with funds provided by Michael R. Kaplan, M.D., Gary B. Sokol, and the Horace W. Goldsmith Foundation

Uta Barth
(b. Berlin 1958)
8. Ground #30, 1994
Color photograph on panel
22 x 18 x 2 in.
(55.9 x 45.7 x 5.1 cm)
Collection Gary and Tracy Mezzatesta
9. Ground #66, 1996
Color photograph on panel
19½ x 20½ x 2 in.
(49.5 x 52.1 x 5.1 cm)
Courtesy of the artist; Acme, Santa Monica, California; and Tanya Bonakdar Gallery, New York
10. Ground #74, 1996
Color photograph on panel
18 x 22½ x 2 in.
(45.7 x 57.2 x 5.1 cm)
Collection Valery Schapiro

Nayland Blake
(b. New York City 1960)
11. Workstation #2, 1988
Steel, leather
38 x 48 x 30 in.
(96.5 x 121.9 x 76.2 cm)
Collection Tom Patchett, Los Angeles

12. Equipment for a Shameful Epic, 1993
Coatrack with costumes and text
86 x 63 x 32 in.
(218.4 x 160 x 81.3 cm)
Courtesy Matthew Marks Gallery, New York
13. Colder + Colder, 1994
Toy bunny head, refrigerator, light
1¼ x 7½ x 5¼ in.
(3.2 x 19.1 x 13.3 cm)
Collection Tom Patchett, Los Angeles
14. El Dorado, 1994
Four stuffed bunnies, three wooden rifles, blindfold, wooden gate
17 x 34 x 12¾ in.
(43.2 x 86.4 x 32.4 cm) approx.
Collection of Peter and Eileen Norton, Santa Monica

Chris Burden
(b. Boston 1946)
15. Relic from Deadman, 1972
Plastic tarp, printed text
Dimensions variable
Collection of the artist
16. Relic from "TV Hijack," 1972
Knife, scabbard, case, printed text
8½ x 10¾ x 6 in.
(21.6 x 27.3 x 15.2 cm)
Orange County Museum of Art, gift of the artist
17. Relic from 747, 1973
Revolver, photograph, printed text
Photograph: 3 x 10 in. (7.6 x 25.4 cm); other dimensions variable
Collection of the artist
18. Sculpture in Three Parts, 1974
Three black-and-white photographs, printed text
8 x 10 in. (20.3 x 25.4 cm) each
Collection of the artist

Vija Celmins

(b. Riga, Latvia, 1938)
19. Time Magazine Cover (Watts Riots), 1965
Oil on canvas
14 x 17 in. (35.6 x 43.2 cm)
Collection of Harold Cook, Ph.D.
20. Tulip Car #1, 1966
Oil on canvas
26 x 36 in. (66 x 91.4 cm) framed
Collection of The Edward R. Broida Trust, Palm Beach, Florida

Bruce Conner

(b. McPherson, Kansas, 1933)
21. Prints, 1974
Mixed media, steel office lockbox containing documents, including a photocopied "edition" of twenty sets of fingerprints
2½ x 16 x 10½ in.
(6.4 x 40.6 x 26.7 cm)
Courtesy Kohn Turner Gallery, Los Angeles, and PZK Contemporary Fine Art, Palo Alto

Eileen Cowin

(b. Brooklyn, New York, 1947)
22. Untitled, 1997
Cibachrome print
50 x 40 in. (127 x 101.6 cm)
Collection of the artist

John Divola

(b. Santa Monica, California, 1949)
23. Los Angeles International Airport, Noise Abatement Zone, Forced Entry (76FES29i), 1976
Black-and-white photograph
14 x 14 in. (35.6 x 35.6 cm)
Collection of the artist
24. Los Angeles International Airport, Noise Abatement Zone, Forced Entry (76FES129e), 1976
Black-and-white photograph
14 x 14 in. (35.6 x 35.6 cm)
Collection of the artist
25. Los Angeles International Airport, Noise Abatement Zone, Forced Entry (76FES15i#2), 1976
Black-and-white photograph
14 x 14 in. (35.6 x 35.6 cm)
Collection of the artist

97. Marcel Duchamp; *Etant Donnes: 1er La Chute d'Eau; 2^e Le Gaz d'Eclairage*, 1946–66; mixed-media assemblage; 95½ x 70 in. (242.5 x 177.8 cm); Philadelphia Museum of Art, gift of the Cassandra Foundation.

26. Los Angeles International Airport, Noise Abatement Zone, Forced Entry (76FES15e#3), 1976
Black-and-white photograph
14 x 14 in. (35.6 x 35.6 cm)
Collection of the artist
27. Broken Furniture and Evidence of Aggression, 1995
Five black-and-white photographs from a series of twelve: Miss Pinkerton, Public Enemy, Lilly Turner, Central Park, and Untitled (broken furniture)
8 x 10 in. (20.3 x 25.4 cm) each
Collection Tom Patchett, Los Angeles

Sam Durant
(b. Seattle 1961)
28. Abandoned House #5, 1995
Mixed media
19½ x 43 x 8½ in.
(49.5 x 109.2 x 21.6 cm)
Collection of the artist; courtesy Blum & Poe, Santa Monica

Vincent Fecteau
(b. Islip, New York, 1969)
29. Shirley Temple Room #8, 1994
Cardboard, tape
10½ x 6 x 12 in.
(26.7 x 15.2 x 30.5 cm)
Courtesy of the artist and Gallery Paule Anglim

Bob Flanagan
(b. New York 1952; d. Los Angeles 1996)
Sheree Rose
(b. Los Angeles 1941)
30. Autopsy, 1994
Single-channel video; made in collaboration with Kirby Dick
23 minutes
Collection of Sheree Rose

Janet Fries
(b. Scranton, Pennsylvania, 1949)
31. Untitled, 1975
Black-and-white photograph
16 x 20 in. (40.6 x 50.8 cm)
Collection of the artist
32. Untitled, 1975
Black-and-white photograph
16 x 20 in. (40.6 x 50.8 cm)
Collection of the artist

David Hammons
(b. Springfield, Illinois, 1943)
33. Admissions Office, 1969
Painted wood; painted glass; metal doorknob, striker, and door stop; acrylic and hardboard base
79 x 34 x 13¾ in.
(200.7 x 86.4 x 34.9 cm);
base: ¾ x 48 x 14½ in.
(1.9 x 121.9 x 36.8 cm)
Collection California Afro-American Museum Foundation

Lyle Ashton Harris
(b. Bronx, New York, 1965)
34. The Watering Hole VI, 1996
Duraflex print
40 x 30 in. (101.6 x 76.2 cm)
Courtesy Jack Tilton Gallery, New York
35. The Watering Hole VIII, 1996
Duraflex print
40 x 30 in. (101.6 x 76.2 cm)
Private collection; courtesy Jack Tilton Gallery, New York

Richard Hawkins
(b. Mexia, Texas, 1961)
36. Poison, 1991
Rubber mask, paper clips, magazine cutouts, nail
Dimensions variable
Private collection, New York; courtesy Feature, Inc., New York

Anthony Hernandez

(b. Los Angeles 1947)

37. Shooting Sites (Angeles National Forest #1), 1988
Cibachrome print
30 x 30 in. (76.2 x 76.2 cm)
Collection of the artist; courtesy Craig Krull Gallery, Santa Monica

38. Untitled (Landscapes for the Homeless #18), 1989
Cibachrome print
30 x 40 in. (76.2 x 101.6 cm)
Collection of the artist; courtesy Craig Krull Gallery, Santa Monica

39. Untitled (Landscapes for the Homeless #24), 1990
Cibachrome print
30 x 60 in. (76.2 x 152.4 cm)
Collection of Bryan and Aileen Cooke; courtesy Craig Krull Gallery, Santa Monica

40. Untitled (Landscapes for the Homeless #62), 1990
Cibachrome print
42 x 54 in. (106.7 x 137.2 cm)
Collection of the artist; courtesy Craig Krull Gallery, Santa Monica

Mike Kelley

(b. Detroit 1954)

41. Eviscerated Corpse, 1989
Cloth animals, found, stuffed, and sewn
71½ x 99½ x 166 in.
(181.6 x 252.7 x 421.6 cm)
The Art Institute of Chicago; gift of the Lannan Foundation

42. Yarn #3, 1990
Blanket, yarn
3 x 34 x 91 in.
(7.6 x 86.4 x 231.1 cm)
Courtesy the artist and Metro Pictures

Edward Kienholz

(b. Fairfield, Washington, 1927; d. Hope, Idaho, 1994)

Nancy Reddin Kienholz

(b. Los Angeles 1943)

43. Sawdy, 1971
Car door, mirrored window, automotive lacquer, polyester resin, silkscreen, fluorescent light, galvanized sheet metal
39½ x 36 x 7 in.

98. Sophie Calle; *La Filature*, 1981; black-and-white photograph; courtesy the artist.

(100.3 x 91.4 x 17.8 cm)
Collection Gemini G.E.L., Los
Angeles
**44. White Easel with Machine
Pistol,** 1975
Mixed media
96½ x 90 x 36 in.
(245.1 x 228.6 x 91.4 cm)
Collection of Nancy Reddin
Kienholz; courtesy of L.A. Louver
Gallery, Venice, California

Barry Le Va
(b. Long Beach, California, 1941)
**45. Shatterscatter (Within the
Series of Layered / Pattern
Acts),** 1968–71
Glass sheets
3½ x 82 x 62 in.
(8.9 x 208.3 x 157.5 cm)
The Museum of Contemporary
Art, Los Angeles, gift of Ileana
Sonnabend

Sharon Lockhart
(b. Norwood, Massachusetts, 1964)
46. Julia Thomas, 1995
Two Ektacolor prints
48 x 60 in. (121.9 x 152.4 cm) each
framed
The Eli Broad Family Foundation,
Santa Monica
47. Untitled, 1996
Cibachrome print
63 x 50⅛ in. (160 x 127.3 cm) framed
Private collection; courtesy Blum
& Poe, Santa Monica

James Luna
(b. Orange, California, 1950)
48. The Tribal Identity, 1995
Mixed-media installation
72 x 120 x 120 in.
(182.9 x 304.8 x 304.8 cm)
Collection of the artist

Monica Majoli
(b. Los Angeles 1963)
49. Untitled, 1990
Oil on wood
5 x 17½ x 1½ in.
(12.7 x 44.5 x 3.8 cm)
Collection of the artist
50. Untitled, 1990
Oil on wood
12 x 12 in. (30.5 x 30.5 cm)
Private collection, Hollywood

Mike Mandel
(b. 1950)
Larry Sultan
(b. Brooklyn, New York, 1946)
51. Evidence, 1977
Ten gelatin-silver prints by
anonymous photographers from a
series of seventy-nine
8 x 10 in. (20.3 x 25.4 cm) each
Center for Creative Photography,
The University of Arizona

Paul McCarthy
(b. Salt Lake City 1945)
52. Santa Chocolate Shop,
1996–97
Mixed-media installation
192 x 144 x 144 in.
(487.7 x 365.8 x 365.8 cm) overall;
chimney: 24 x 24 x 168 in.
(61 x 61 x 426.7 cm)
Luhring Augustine, New York

Richard Misrach
(b. Los Angeles 1949)
53. Dead Animals #362, 1987–89
Dye-coupler color photograph
40 x 50 in. (101.6 x 127 cm)
Courtesy Jan Kesner Gallery
54. Playboy #38 (Warhol),
1989–91
Chromogenic color print
30 x 40 in. (76.2 x 101.6 cm)

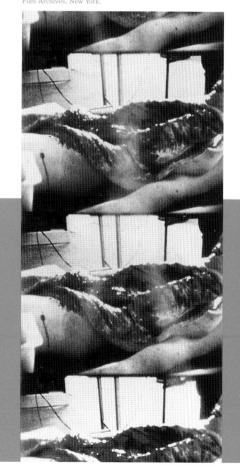

99. Stan Brakhage; *The Act of Seeing with One's Own Eyes*, 1971; black-and-white still from color film; courtesy the artist and Anthology Film Archives, New York.

Courtesy Fraenkel Gallery,
San Francisco
55. Playboy #42 (Rambo),
1989–91
Dye-coupler color photograph
40 x 50 in. (101.6 x 127 cm)
Courtesy Curt Marcus Gallery,
New York
56. Playboy #90 (Hole in the
Mouth), 1989–91
Dye-coupler color photograph
40 x 50 in. (101.6 x 127 cm)
Courtesy Curt Marcus Gallery,
New York
57. Office, Hangar of the Enola
Gay, 1990
Dye-coupler color photograph
20 x 24 in. (50.8 x 61 cm)
Courtesy Jan Kesner Gallery

Bruce Nauman
(b. Fort Worth, Indiana, 1941)
58. Burning Small Fires, 1968
Bound booklet of black-and-white
photographs of Ed Ruscha's book
entitled Various Small Fires
12⅝ x 9⅝ x ⅛ in. (32.1 x 24.4 x 1.6
cm) closed; 49 x 36½ in. (124.5 x
92.7 cm) unfolded
Collection of Edward Ruscha
59. Dead Center, 1969
Steel
3 x 15 x 15 in. (7.6 x 38.1 x 38.1 cm)
The Solomon R. Guggenheim
Museum, New York, gift of the
Theodoran Foundation, 1969

Robert Overby
(b. Harvey, Illinois, 1935;
d. Los Angeles 1993)
60. Door with Hole, Second
Floor, 4 August 1971, 1971
Latex rubber
80½ x 34 in. (204.5 x 86.4 cm)
Courtesy Linda Burnham and

Jessica Fredericks Gallery,
New York
61. #208, East Hall Wall, Third
Floor (Gray Wall), 4 August 1971,
1971
Latex rubber
104 x 186½ in. (264.2 x 473.7 cm)
Courtesy Linda Burnham
and Jessica Fredericks Gallery,
New York

Nancy Reese
(b. Rock Hill, South Carolina, 1949)
62. El Señor, 1990
Oil and enamel on canvas
96 x 72 in. (243.8 x 182.9 cm)
Collection of Daniel Melnick, Los
Angeles

Michelle Rollman
(b. Denver 1967)
63. Untitled (Instrument Case),
1995
Mixed media
18 x 32 x 14 in.
(45.7 x 81.3 x 35.6 cm)
Collection of the artist; courtesy
Gallery Paule Anglim

Edward Ruscha
(b. Omaha, Nebraska, 1937)
64. Los Angeles County Museum
on Fire, 1965–68
Oil on canvas
55 x 135 in. (139.7 x 342.9 cm)
framed
Collection Hirshhorn Museum
and Sculpture Garden,
Smithsonian Institution; gift of
Joseph H. Hirshhorn, 1972
65. Royal Road Test, 1967
Made in collaboration with Mason
Williams and Patrick Blackwell
Spiral-bound, offset-printed
artist's book

9½ x 6½ x ¼ in. (24.1 x 16.5 x .6 cm)
Department of Special
Collections, UCLA University
Research Library
66. Three Murders, 1981
Oil on canvas
20 x 159 in. (50.8 x 403.9 cm)
Collection of the artist

Alexis Smith
(b. Los Angeles 1949)
**67. All the Simple Old
Fashioned Charm,** 1984
Lacquered wood chair, stick-on
letters
34 x 17¼ x 19½ in.
(86.4 x 43.8 x 49.5 cm)
Courtesy Margo Leavin Gallery,
Los Angeles

George Stone
(b. Los Angeles 1946)
**68. Unknown, Unwanted,
Unconscious, Untitled,** 1993
Mixed-media installation, five
elements
18 x 72 x 24 in.

(45.7 x 182.9 x 61 cm) each
Ruth and Jake Bloom and Judy
and Stuart Spence; courtesy of
the artist

Jeffrey Vallance
(b. Torrance, California, 1955)
69. Blinky Specimen Jar, 1988
Glass jar, liquids
5 x 3 x 3 in. (12.7 x 7.6 x 7.6 cm)
Courtesy the artist
70. Run Over Art Shipment,
1990
Cardboard, packing tape, tire
treads, documents
31¾ x 24½ in. (80.6 x 62.2 cm)
Courtesy the artist
**71. Cloth Penetrated by the
Holy Lance,** 1992
Cotton
11½ x 11½ in. (29.2 x 29.2 cm)
Courtesy the artist
72. La Santa Lancia, 1992
Iron, brass, steel, and leather in
Plexiglas and wood case
1 x 20 x 3½ in. (2.5 x 50.8 x 8.9 cm)
Collection of the artist

100. Christo; *Wrapping a
Woman*, 1963; photographed
during the film *Wrapping a
Woman,* by Charles Wilp,
London, 1963. Photo by Anthony
Haden-Guest. ©1963 Christo.

Lenders to the Exhibition

Terry Allen
The Art Institute of Chicago
John Baldessari
Uta Barth
Ruth and Jake Bloom
Blum & Poe, Santa Monica
Chris Burden
Linda Burnham
Nao Bustamonte
California Afro-American
   Museum Foundation
Center for Creative
   Photography, The University
   of Arizona
Harold Cook, Ph.D.
Bryan and Aileen Cooke
Eileen Cowin
Curt Marcus Gallery,
   New York
John Divola
The Edward R. Broida Trust,
   Palm Beach, Florida
Feature, Inc., New York
Fraenkel Gallery, San
   Francisco
Janet Fries
Gallery Paule Anglim
Gemini G.E.L., Los Angeles
Robert H. Halff
Lyle Ashton Harris
Anthony Hernandez
Hirshhorn Museum and
   Sculpture Garden,
   Smithsonian Institution,
   Washington, D.C.
Jack Hanley Gallery
Nancy Reddin Kienholz
Kohn Turner Gallery,
   Los Angeles
Los Angeles County Museum
   of Art
James Luna
Monica Majoli
Margo Leavin Gallery, Los
   Angeles
Matthew Marks Gallery, New
   York
Paul McCarthy
Daniel Melnick, Los Angeles
Metro Pictures
Gary and Tracy Mezzatesta

Richard Misrach
Museum of Contemporary
   Art, Los Angeles
Peter and Eileen Norton,
   Santa Monica
Orange County Museum of
   Art, Newport Beach,
   California
Tom Patchett, Los Angeles
Sheree Rose
Edward Ruscha
Valery Shapiro
Solomon R. Guggenheim
   Museum, New York
Sonnabend Gallery, New York
Judy and Stuart Spence
George Stone
UCLA University Research
   Library, Department of
   Special Collections
Jeffrey Vallance

Private collection (4)

101. Rachel Whiteread; *Untitled (Amber Slab)*, 1991; rubber cast of mortuary slab; 81 x 31 x 4½ in. (205.7 x 78.7 x 11.4 cm); courtesy Luhring Augustine Gallery, New York.

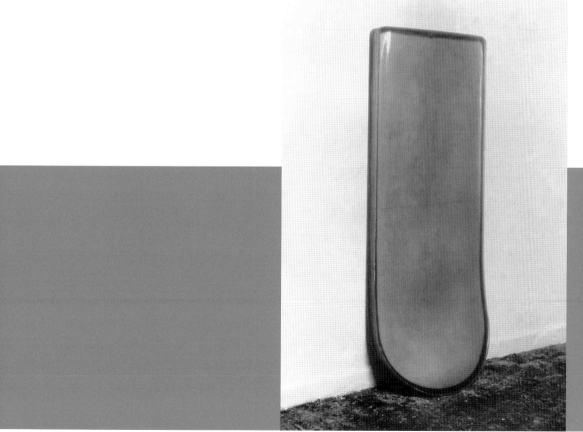

Index

Numbers in **boldface** refer to pages with illustrations.

102. Andy Warhol; *Red Disaster* (first panel), 1963; silkscreen: ink on synthetic polymer paint on linen; 93 x 80¼ in. (236.2 x 203.9 cm); Museum of Fine Arts, Boston. Charles H. Bayley Picture and Painting Fund.

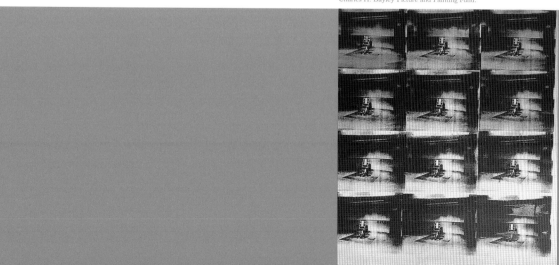

103. Mike Kelley; *Torture Table*, 1992; wood, buckets, knife, plastic pillow; 36½ x 96 x 48 in. (92.7 x 243.8 x 121.9 cm); courtesy the artist and Metro Pictures.

Fellows of Contemporary Art

The Fellows of Contemporary Art, founded in 1975, is a nonprofit, independent corporation that supports contemporary art in California by initiating and sponsoring exhibitions of emerging and mid-career artists at selected institutions. The Fellows does not make grants to individuals or maintain a permanent facility or collection. In addition to sponsoring exhibitions, the Fellows' membership participates in a very active program of domestic and international tours and educational programs.

Grace and Richard Narver
Lura and Robert Newhouse
E. Louise Newquist
Sandra Kline Nichols and
  Peter Nichols
Eileen and Peter Norton
Cathie and David Partridge
Suzanne and Theodore Paulson
Joan Payden
Putter and Blair Pence
Audree and Standish Penton
Ellie and Frank Person
Tina Petra and Ken Wong
Peggy Phelps and
  Nelson Leonard
Linda and Reese Polesky
Dallas Price
Kathy Reges and
  Richard Carlson
Joan B. Rehnborg
Carol and John Richards
Debby and Bill Richards
Gayle and Edward Roski
June W. Schuster
Gretchen and David Seager
Deborah Sharpe and
  Henry Finkelstein
Ann and George Smith
Annette and Russell
  Dymock Smith
Miriam Smith and
  Doug Greene
Gwen Laurie and
  Howard Smits
Penny and Ted Sonnenschein
Judith and Milton Stark

Laurie Smits Staude
Margarita and
  David Steinmetz
Clara and Jason Stevens
Ginny and Richard Stever
Arthur Strick
Ann E. Summers
Joan and Louis Swartz
Janet and Dennis Tani
Laney and Thomas Techentin
Elinor and Rubin Turner
Lois and Jim Ukropina
Jolly Urner
Donna Vaccarino
Carolyn and Bob Volk
Cindy and Jim Wagner
Magda and Frederick
  Waingrow
George F. Wick
Biji and Toby Wilcox
Mili Julia Wild
Bonnie and Jack Wilke
Cynthia and Eric Wittenberg
Maybelle Bayly Wolfe
Laura-Lee and Robert Woods

104. Nayland Blake, *Workstation #2*, 1988 (cat. no. 11).

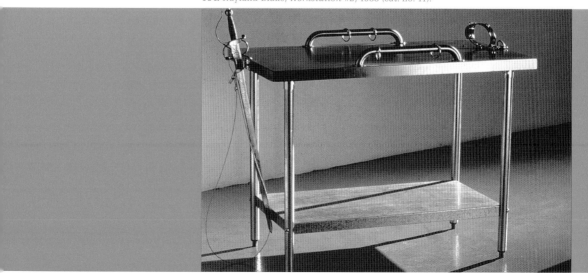

Exhibition History

1976

Ed Moses Drawings,
1958–1976
Frederick S. Wight Art Gallery,
University of California, Los
Angeles
July 13–August 15, 1976
Catalogue with essay by
Joseph Masheck

1977

Unstretched
Surfaces/Surfaces Libres
Los Angeles Institute of
Contemporary Art
November 5–December 16,
1977
Artists: Bernadette Bour,
Jerrold Burchman, Thierry
Delaroyere, Daniel Dezeuze,
Charles Christopher Hill,
Christian Jaccard, Allan
McCollum, Jean-Michel
Meurice, Jean-Pierre
Pincemin, Peter Plagens,
Tom Wudl, Richard Yokomi
Catalogue with essays by
Jean-Luc Bordeaux, Pontus
Hulten, and Alfred
Pacquement

1978–80

Wallace Berman
Retrospective
Otis Art Institute Gallery, Los
Angeles
October 24–November 25, 1978
Exhibition traveled to: Fort
Worth Art Museum, Fort
Worth, Texas; University Art
Museum, University of
California, Berkeley; Seattle
Art Museum
Catalogue with essays by
Robert Duncan and David
Meltzer
Supported by a grant from
the National Endowment for
the Arts, Washington, D.C.,
a federal agency

1979–80

Vija Celmins: A Survey
Exhibition
Newport Harbor Art Museum,
Newport Beach, California
December 15, 1979–February 3,
1980

Exhibition traveled to: The
Arts Club of Chicago; The
Hudson River Museum,
Yonkers, New York; The
Corcoran Gallery of Art,
Washington, D.C.
Catalogue with essay by
Susan C. Larsen
Supported by a grant from
the National Endowment for
the Arts, Washington, D.C.,
a federal agency

1980

Variations: Five Los Angeles
Painters
University Art Galleries,
University of Southern
California, Los Angeles
October 20–November 23, 1980
Artists: Robert Ackerman, Ed
Gilliam, George Rodart, Don
Suggs, Norton Wisdom
Catalogue with essay by
Susan C. Larsen

1981–82

Craig Kauffman:
Comprehensive Survey,
1957–1980
La Jolla Museum of
Contemporary Art, La Jolla,
California
March 14–May 3, 1981
Exhibition traveled to:
Elvehjem Museum of Art,
University of Wisconsin,
Madison; Anderson Gallery,
Virginia Commonwealth
University, Richmond; The
Oakland Museum, Oakland,
California
Catalogue with essay by
Robert McDonald
Supported by a grant from
the National Endowment for
the Arts, Washington, D.C.,
a federal agency

1981–82

Paul Wonner: Abstract
Realist
San Francisco Museum of
Modern Art
October 1–November 22, 1981
Exhibition traveled to:
Marion Koogler McNay Art
Institute, San Antonio, Texas;
Los Angeles Municipal Art
Gallery

Catalogue with essay by
George W. Neubert

1982–83

Changing Trends: Content
and Style: Twelve Southern
California Painters
Laguna Beach Museum of Art,
Laguna Beach, California
November 18, 1982–January 3,
1983
Exhibition traveled to: Los
Angeles Institute of
Contemporary Art
Artists: Robert Ackerman,
Caron Colvin, Scott Grieger,
Marvin Harden, James
Hayward, Ron Linden, John
Miller, Pierre Picot, George
Rodart, Don Suggs, David
Trowbridge, Tom Wudl
Catalogue with essays by
Francis Colpitt, Christopher
Knight, Peter Plagens, and
Robert Smith

1983

Variations II: Seven Los
Angeles Painters
Gallery at the Plaza, Security
Pacific National Bank, Los
Angeles
May 8–June 30, 1983
Artists: Roy Dowell, Kim
Hubbard, William Mahan,
David Lawson, Janet
McCloud, Richard Sedivy,
Hye Sook
Catalogue with essay by
Constance Mallinson

1984

Martha Alf Retrospective
Los Angeles Municipal Art
Gallery
March 6–April 1, 1984
Exhibition traveled to:
San Francisco Art Institute
Catalogue with essay by
Suzanne Muchnic

1985

Sunshine and Shadow:
Recent Painting in Southern
California
Fisher Gallery, University of
Southern California, Los
Angeles
January 15–February 23, 1985
Artists: Robert Ackerman,

Richard Baker, William Brice, Karen Carson, Lois Colette, Ronald Davis, Richard Diebenkorn, John Eden, Llyn Foulkes, Charles Garabedian, Candice Gawne, Joe Goode, James Hayward, Roger Herman, Charles Christopher Hill, Craig Kauffman, Gary Lang, Dan McCleary, Arnold Mesches, John M. Miller, Ed Moses, Margit Omar, Marc Pally, Pierre Picot, Peter Plagens, Luis Serrano, Reesey Shaw, Ernest Silva, Tom Wudl Catalogue with essay by Susan C. Larsen

1985–86
James Turrell
The Museum of Contemporary Art, Los Angeles
November 13, 1985–February 9, 1986
A book entitled *Occluded Front: James Turrell* was published in conjunction with the exhibition. It includes contributions by Craig Adcock, Julia Brown, John Coplans, Edy de Wilde, Craig Hodgetts, Lucebert, Count Giuseppe Panza di Biumo, Jim Simmerman, James Turrell, and Theodore F. Wolff.

1986
William Brice
The Museum of Contemporary Art, Los Angeles
September 1–October 19, 1986
Exhibition traveled to: Grey Art Gallery and Study Center, New York University
Full-color catalogue with essay by Richard Armstrong

1987
Variations III: Emerging Artists in Southern California
Los Angeles Contemporary Exhibitions
April 22–May 31, 1987
Exhibition traveled to: Fine Arts Gallery, University of California, Irvine; Art Gallery, California State University, Northridge, California
Artists: Alvaro Asturias/ John Castagna, Hildegarde Duane/David Lamelas, Tom Knechtel, Joyce Lightbody, Julie Medwedeff, Ihnsoon Nam, Ed Nunnery, Patti Podesta, Deborah Small, Rena Small, Linda Ann Stark
Catalogue with essay by Melinda Wortz

1987–88
Perpetual Motion
Santa Barbara Museum of Art, Santa Barbara, California
November 17, 1987–January 24, 1988
Artists: Karen Carson, Margaret Nielsen, John Rogers, Tom Wudl
Catalogue with essay by Betty Turnbull

1988
Jud Fine
La Jolla Museum of Contemporary Art, La Jolla, California
August 19–October 2, 1988
Exhibition traveled to: De Saisset Museum, Santa Clara University, Santa Clara, California
Catalogue with essays by Madeleine Grynstejn and Ronald J. Onorato
Travel supported by a grant from the National Endowment for the Arts, Washington, D.C., a federal agency

1989–90
The Pasadena Armory Show 1989
The Armory Center for the Arts, Pasadena, California

105. Ilya Kabakov; *Artist's Despair or Conspiracy of the Untalented*, 1994; three paintings (framed), broken glass, axe, texts, table and chairs, wood barrier; paintings: 49 x 71 in. (124.5 x 180.3 cm) each; installation dimensions variable; private collection; courtesy Rosamund Felsen Gallery, Santa Monica.

November 2, 1989–January 31, 1990
Artists: Carole Caroompas, Karen Carson, Michael Davis, James Doolin, Scott Grieger, Raul Guerrero, William Leavitt, Jerry McMillan, Michael C. McMillen, Margit Omar, John Outterbridge, Ann Page, John Valadez
Catalogue with essay by Dave Hickey and curatorial statement by Noel Korten

1990
Lita Albuquerque: Reflections
Santa Monica Museum of Art, Santa Monica, California
January 19–April 1, 1990
Catalogue with essay by Jan Butterfield and interview with Lita Albuquerque by curator Henry Hopkins

1991
Facing the Finish: Some Recent California Art
San Francisco Museum of Modern Art
September 20–December 1, 1991
Exhibition traveled to: Santa Barbara Contemporary Arts Forum, Santa Barbara, California; Art Center College of Design, Pasadena, California
Artists: Nayland Blake, Jerome Caja, Jim Campbell, David Kremers, Rachel Lachowicz, James Luna, Jorge Pardo, Sarah Seager, Christopher Williams, Millie Wilson
Catalogue with essays by John Caldwell and Bob Riley

1991–93
Roland Reiss: A Seventeen-Year Survey
Los Angeles Municipal Art Gallery
November 19, 1991–January 19, 1992
Exhibition traveled to: University of Arizona Museum of Art, Tucson; The Neuberger Museum of Art, State University of New York

at Purchase; Palm Springs Desert Museum, Palm Springs, California
Catalogue with essays by Betty Ann Brown, Robert Dawidoff, Merle Schipper, Richard Smith, and Buzz Spector

1992–94
Proof: Los Angeles Art and the Photograph, 1960–1980
Laguna Art Museum, Laguna Beach, California
October 31, 1992–January 17, 1993
Exhibition traveled to: De Cordova Museum and Sculpture Park, Lincoln, Massachusetts; The Friends of Photography, Ansel Adams Center, San Francisco; Montgomery Museum of Fine Arts, Montgomery, Alabama; Tampa Museum of Art; Des Moines Art Center
Artists: Terry Allen, Eleanor Antin, John Baldessari, Wallace Berman, George Blakely, Ellen Brooks, Gillian Brown, Robert E. Brown, Gary Burns, Jack Butler, Carl Cheng, Eileen Cowin, Robert Cumming, Darryl Curran, Lou Brown DiGiulio, John Divola, Robert Fichter, Robbert Flick, Llyn Foulkes, Vida Freeman, Judith Golden, Susan Haller, Robert Heinecken, George Herms, Dennis Hopper, Suda House, Douglas Huebler, Steve Kahn, Barbara Kasten, Edward Kienholz, Ellen Land-Weber, Victor Landweber, Paul McCarthy, Jerry McMillan, Virgil Mirano, Stanley Mock, Susan Rankaitis, Allen Ruppersberg, Edward Ruscha, Ilene Segalove, Allan Sekula, Kenneth Shorr, Alexis Smith, Michael Stone, Todd Walker, William Wegman
Catalogue with essay by Charles Desmarais
Supported by a grant from the National Endowment for the Arts, Washington, D.C., a federal agency.

1993–94
Kim Abeles, Encyclopedia Persona: A Fifteen-Year Survey
Santa Monica Museum of Art, Santa Monica, California
September 23–December 6, 1993
Exhibition traveled to: Fresno Art Museum, California; Southeastern Center for Contemporary Art, Winston-Salem Forum, Saint Louis
USIA Arts America Program organized a tour through Latin America for 1996: National Museum of Fine Arts, Santiago; Complejo Cultural Recoleta, Buenos Aires; Museum of Modern Art, Rio de Janeiro; Museum of Modern Art, Caracas
Catalogue with essays by Kim Abeles, Lucinda Barnes, and Karen Moss
Additional support by grants from the Andy Warhol Foundation for the Visual Arts, Inc.; the Peter Norton Family Foundation; and the J. Paul Getty Trust Fund for Visual Arts, a fund of the California Community Foundation

1994–95
Plane/Structures
Otis Art Gallery, Otis College of Art and Design, Los Angeles
September 10–November 5, 1994
Exhibition traveled to: Renaissance Society, Chicago; Pittsburgh Center for the Arts, Pennsylvania; Center for the Arts, Wesleyan University, Connecticut; Nevada Institute for Contemporary Art, Las Vegas
Artists: Fandra Chang, Mary Corse, Caren Furbeyre, Jeremy Gilbert-Rolfe, James Hayward, Maxwell Hendler, Scot Heywood, Linda Hudson, Liz Larner, John M. Miller, Jim Richards, Roy Thurston, Carolee Toon, Alan Wayne, Jonathan White, Pae White

Catalogue with essays by
Dave Hickey, David Pagel, and
Joe Scanlan
Travel supported by a grant
from the Lannan Foundation;
additional support from the
Peter Norton Family
Foundation

1995–96

Llyn Foulkes: Between a
Rock and a Hard Place
Laguna Art Museum, Laguna
Beach, California
October 27, 1995–January 21,
1996
Exhibition traveled to: The
Contemporary Art Center,
Cincinnati; The Oakland
Museum, Oakland, California;
Palm Springs Desert Museum,
Palm Springs, California
Catalogue with essays by
Rosetta Brooks and Marilu
Knode

Video Series

**Videos are produced
and directed by
Joe Leonardi, Long Beach
Museum of Art Video
Annex, for the Fellows of
Contemporary Art.**

Red Is Green: Jud Fine, 1988
*Horace Bristol:
Photojournalist,* 1989
*Altering Discourse: The Works
of Helen and Newton
Harrison,* 1989
*Frame and Context: Richard
Ross,* 1989
*Experience: Perception,
Interpretation, Illusion (The
Pasadena Armory Show
1989),* 1989
*Secrets, Dialogs, Revelations:
The Art of Betye and Alison
Saar,* 1990
Lita Albuquerque: Reflections,
1990
Los Angeles Murals, 1990
Stretching the Canvas (compi-
lation tape narrated by Peter
Sellars), 1990
Michael Todd: Jazz, 1990
Waterworks, 1990
*Roland Reiss: A Seventeen-
Year Survey,* 1991
Kim Abeles, 1993

106. Vito Acconci; *Seedbed*, 1972; installation/performance at Sonnabend Gallery, New York, January 15–29, 1972; wooden ramp and loudspeaker; courtesy Barbara Gladstone Gallery, New York.

Photography Credits

We wish to thank the owners and custodians for permitting the reproduction of the works of art in their collections. The photographers and/or sources of the illustrations, whose courtesy is gratefully acknowledged, are listed below.

107. William Anastasi; *West Wall, Dwan Main Gallery*, 1966 (first exhibited in 1967); oil silkscreen on canvas; 85½ x 157 in. (217.2 x 398.8 cm); courtesy the artist.

Ralph Rugoff is an independent curator and critic and the author of *Circus Americanus* and coauthor of *Paul McCarthy*.

Peter Wollen is professor of film at the University of California, Los Angeles, and the author of numerous books on art history and film theory, including *Raiding the Icebox: Reflections o̶* *Twentieth-Century Culture.*

Anthony Vidler has taught at Princeton University, UCLA, and Cornell University author of many book$ on architectural theory and history, including *The Architectu̶*